Strategic
Pastoral
Counseling

Strategic Pastoral Counseling

A Short-Term Structured Model

SECOND EDITION

David G. Benner, Ph.D., C.Psych.

Baker Academic

A Division of Baker Book House Co
Grand Rapids, Michigan 49516

Published by Baker Academic
a division of Baker Book House Company
P.O. Box 6287, Grand Rapids, MI 49516-6287
www.bakeracademic.com

Second printing, May 2004

Printed in the United States of America

                   Library of Congress Cataloging-in-Publication Data
Benner, David G.
     Strategic pastoral counseling : a short-term structured model /
David G. Benner.—2nd ed.
          p.   cm.
     Includes bibliographical references.
     ISBN 0-8010-2631-8 (pbk. alk. paper)
     1. Pastoral counseling. 2. Short-term counseling—Religious
aspects—Christianity. I. Title.
BV4012.2.B366 2003
253.5—dc21   2003041949

While all the stories and examples in this book are based on real people and events, names and identifying details have been altered to protect the privacy of the individuals involved. Some illustrations are composites of different persons and situations.

Contents

Preface

Eleven years ago when I offered the first edition of this book, I did so with quite modest expectations. Pastoral counseling was firmly wed to a traditional long-term counseling model. I had long been convinced that pastors could much better fit counseling within their pastoral ministries as a whole by making it brief and focused. However, most pastors whom I encouraged to do so responded in a way that made it clear that a psychologist could never really understand the realities of pastoral life and practice and that the sort of problems they encountered simply demanded long-term counseling.

All that has changed enormously in the past decade. Numerous models of short-term pastoral counseling now exist, and the argument has largely been won that short-term counseling best fits the mix of responsibilities encountered by pastors who counsel.

Changes in this edition are based on feedback from pastors who have adopted *Strategic Pastoral Counseling*, many of whom have now used it for the past decade. Nigerian, Philippine, and Korean editions have provided helpful response from several cross-cultural applications, and the comments of a number of professors in seminaries who have been using the book as a text, as well as from students studying it, have also been invaluable.

Completely rewritten and revised, this second edition includes more case examples, a new appendix on ethical considerations, and updated suggestions for additional reading. A new first chapter places pastoral counseling into a much broader context of Christian soul care than was present in the first edition. This includes a discussion of the relationship between pastoral counseling and spiritual direction. Chapter 2 now includes a more extended case for brief pastoral counseling and refers to some of the other models that are available. The place of both homework and spiritual focus in strategic pastoral counseling get more extended treatment in chapter 3, as does the use of congregational and other spiritual resources. And chapter 6 presents a new case illustration of single-session strategic pastoral counseling.

The primary audience for this edition once again remains pastors who counsel in addition to their other pastoral-care responsibilities. They, along with seminarians who are preparing for such a role and nonclerical counselors who offer their services from within the church and as an integral part of its ministry, were in the forefront of my mind as I have worked on this revision. My secondary audience includes pastoral counselors whose counseling is not part of a parish ministry but may be offered in a hospital, interdenominational or interfaith community counseling center, or private practice. Some of what I present may be basic to those within this group who have completed more advanced counseling or clinical pastoral education training. However, my hope is that the information will also serve individuals within this group by highlighting the spiritual aspects of brief pastoral counseling practice that characterize strategic pastoral counseling.

Preface to the First Edition

With over three hundred different English language books on pastoral care and counseling currently in print, it is quite reasonable to ask why one more is needed. An adequate justification for a new book must be based on the demonstration of both the importance of the subject matter and the unique contribution that the book will make. Let me briefly state, therefore, why I think this present book is both important and unique.

Since you are reading this preface, you probably need no further convincing about the importance of pastoral counseling. And yet, this is the place to begin. The importance of pastoral care and counseling is grounded in the centrality of the proclamation of the Word of God in Christian ministry. While this fundamental nature of proclamation would probably be readily acknowledged by most clergy, Aden suggests that the common understanding of what this means is too narrow (Aden 1988). He argues that we tend to equate proclamation with preaching, although, more correctly understood, it involves much more than the mere imparting of information and includes a much broader range of activities than preaching. Proclamation involves not only a communication of an event but also an actualization of this event. Proclamation delivers or makes real what it talks about, and it does this in the present moment and experience of the one who receives the proclamation. Properly understood, therefore, proclamation brings individuals into direct, immediate, and personal contact with God's Word. While this is the essence of all good preaching, it should also be the foundation of a broad range of other pastoral activities.

Understood in this way, pastoral care and counseling are legitimate parts of Christian ministry because they provide a unique opportunity for God's Word to be spoken to the specific life experiences of the person seeking pastoral help. Pastoral counseling should never be a matter of simply preaching to someone after hearing his or her story. Rather, it involves relating the Word to specific needs and life experiences and embodying it in what Aden has called "a living relationship of loving service" (Aden 1988, 40). It is a form of proclamation that often cannot be performed equally well by any other act of ministry, and for this reason, it has had a central and important role in the long tradition of Christian soul care.

The importance of pastoral counseling is reinforced by the fact that for most pastors it is not an optional activity but one that the needs and demands of their parishioners regularly necessitate. Research indicates that the average pastor spends between six and eight hours each week in counseling. Very few pastors are able to avoid counseling responsibilities altogether, and those that do seem generally to be on the staff of churches where others are providing these services. For the vast majority of pastors, some counseling responsibility is a given that cannot be avoided. The needs of their parishioners demand that they see people in counseling relationships, whether they are adequately prepared to do so or not.

And how well prepared for counseling do most pastors judge themselves to be? In background research for the present volume, only 13 percent of the pastors contacted reported that they felt adequately prepared for their counseling responsibilities; 87 percent reported a need for further training in pastoral counseling. Both seminary training and existing books on pastoral counseling leave most pastors unprepared for counseling. This lack of preparation is obviously a major reason as to why so many pastors reported that counseling is frustrating and unfulfilling. They know counseling is an important part of their overall responsibilities and therefore feel guilty if it is minimized or ignored. But at the same time, they also feel inadequate in the face of its demands. Unavoidable, counseling quickly becomes a source of frustration and dissatisfaction.

The pastors contacted were asked what sort of help they needed to prepare them better for their work in pastoral counseling. They said that if books on pastoral counseling are to be helpful, they must be much more practical than is usually the case. Books on the theology of pastoral care or the theory of pastoral counseling may look good on the shelf, but they provide little help when a disturbed parishioner enters the office. To be helpful, books must tell pastors specifically what to do with those they face in counseling sessions. General principles are simply not good enough.

Strategic pastoral counseling is a model of counseling that has been specifically designed in response to this request for practical help for pastors who counsel. The term *strategic* emphasizes the fact that the approach is highly focused, the pastor being provided with clear goals and strategies for each of the five recommended sessions. This recommended maximum of five sessions fits both what pastors say is the actual length of most of their counseling relationships and what they think is the amount of time they can give to counseling and still meet the other demands of their schedules. The focus of strategic pastoral counseling is the parishioner's spiritual functioning, and the parishioner's life and present struggles are the context in which these spiritual matters should be discerned. Strategic pastoral counseling is also explicitly Christian, and the use of the unique resources of the Christian life is fully encouraged.

Since as part of their formal training most pastors have limited coursework in pastoral counseling, strategic pastoral counseling does not assume a background in psychology or counseling theory. This book, therefore, avoids jargon, and when technical terms are employed, they are clearly explained. However, the approach does not fail to recognize that most pastors have some experience in counseling and considerable experience in pastoral care. In fact, general ministry and more specialized pastoral-care experience are the assumed foundation for what is presented, and strategic pastoral counseling is positioned as integral to and necessarily consistent with these broader pastoral roles.

Pastoral counseling should be at the very heart of pastoral care and ministry. However, the clinical models of counseling that have often been adopted by pastoral counselors have tended to make counseling into a specialized activity that bears little relationship to other pastoral activities and responsibilities. Strategic pastoral counseling seeks to address this problem by presenting an approach to counseling that, while drawing extensively on the general principles and approaches to counseling that have been developed within therapeutic psychology over the past several decades, takes its form and direction from the pastoral role. It is hoped that it will be of value to those pastors who seek to provide counsel that is congruent not only with their theological commitments and biblical understanding but also with their primary role as ministers of the gospel of Christ.

1

Pastoral Counseling as Soul Care

Although pastors have been providing spiritual counsel as a part of their overall soul-care responsibilities since the earliest days of the church, what we today think of as pastoral counseling is a relatively recent phenomenon. In his *History of Pastoral Care in America* (1983), Holifield dates its development to the first decade of the twentieth century when a group of New England pastors first began to consider how the newly developed procedures of counseling and psychotherapy could be put into spiritual use by the church.

Contemporary pastoral counseling has grown up alongside general psychological counseling—both being fruits of the twentieth-century "triumph of the therapeutic" (Rieff 1966). Attempting to find its identity within this therapeutic culture, pastoral counseling has often experienced tension between the pastoral and the psychological. Some forms of pastoral counseling have borne more resemblance to modern psychotherapy than to historic Christian soul care. Other pastors have sought to distance themselves entirely from psychological counseling, seeking simply to offer biblically based spiritual counsel.

But there is a middle road between mimicking current psychological fads and ignoring the contributions of modern therapeutic psychology. Pastoral counseling can be both distinctively pastoral and psychologically informed. This occurs when it takes its identity from the rich tradition of Christian soul care and integrates appropriate insights of modern therapeutic psychology in a manner that protects both the integrity of the pastoral role and the unique resources of Christian ministry.

Christian Soul Care

The English phrase "care of souls" has its origin in the Latin *cura animarum*. While *cura* is most commonly translated "care," it actually contains the idea of both care and cure. Care refers to actions designed to support the well-being of something or someone. Cure refers to actions designed to restore well-being that has been lost. The Christian church has historically embraced both meanings of *cura* and has understood soul care to involve nurture and support as well as healing and restoration.

But what does it mean to identify the soul as the focus of this care and cure? "Soul" is the most common translation of the Hebrew word *nepesh* and the Greek word *psyche*. Many biblical scholars suggest, however, that a better translation is either "person" or "self." The soul is not a part of a person but his or her total self. We do not have a soul; we are soul—just as we are spirit and we are embodied. A human being is a living and vital whole. "Soul," therefore, refers to the whole person, including the body, but with particular focus on the inner world of thinking, feeling, and willing. Care of souls can thus be understood as the support and restoration of the well-being of a person in his or her depth and totality, with particular concern for the inner life.

Caring for souls is caring for people in ways that not only acknowledge them as persons but also engage and address them in the deepest and most profoundly human aspects of their lives. This is the reason for the priority of the spiritual and psychological aspects of the person's inner world in soul care. It is these aspects of life that mark us most distinctively as human. But genuine soul care is never exclusively focused on any one aspect of a person's being to the exclusion of all others. If care is to be worthy of being called soul care, it must not address parts or focus on problems but engage two or more people with one another to the end of the nurture and growth of the whole person (Benner 1998).

Over the course of its long history, Christian soul care has had varied expressions but has always been a central part of the life and mission of the church. Reviewing this history, Clebsch and Jaekle (1964) note that such care has involved four primary elements: healing, sustaining, reconciling, and guiding. *Healing* involves efforts to help someone overcome an impairment and move toward wholeness. These curative efforts can involve physical healing as well as spiritual healing, but the focus is always the total person, whole and holy. *Sustaining* refers to acts of caring designed to help a hurting person endure and transcend a circumstance in which restoration or recuperation is either impossible or improbable. *Reconciling* refers to efforts to reestablish broken relationships. The presence of this component of care demonstrates the communal, not simply individual, nature of Christian soul care. Finally, *guiding* refers to helping a person make wise choices and thereby grow in spiritual maturity.

Christians seeking to care for the souls of others have heard confessions, given counsel, offered consolation, preached sermons, written books and letters, visited people, developed and run hospitals, organized schools and offered education, and engaged in social and political activities. All these and many more things have been undertaken to the end of what McNeil describes as "the presentation of all people perfect in Christ to God" (McNeil 1951, vii). This suggests that the overarching goal of Christian soul care may be thought of as spiritual formation, the formation of the character of Christ within his people.

Twentieth-century soul care has become narrowed by the clinical and therapeutic approach to persons that has become dominant both inside and outside the church. Care has been largely overshadowed by cure as clergy and laity alike have been displaced by counselors as the preferred providers.

Christian soul care is, however, much too important to be restricted to the curative activities associated with modern clinical therapeutics. It is also much broader than counseling—even pastoral counseling. Understanding where pastoral counseling fits within the spectrum of Christian soul care is essential if it is to fill its distinctive and most important niche.

At least five forms of soul care should be a part of the life of every Christian church: Christian friendship, pastoral ministry, pastoral care, pastoral counseling, and spiritual direction.[1] The continuum that they form is a continuum of specialization—moving from broadest and least specialized to narrowest and most specialized. It is not a continuum of importance. The relationship of these forms of soul care is depicted in figure 1.

Figure 1
The Context of Pastoral Counseling

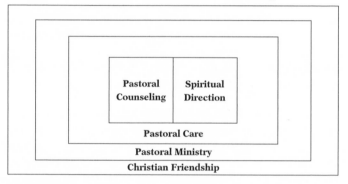

Pastoral Counseling	Spiritual Direction

Pastoral Care

Pastoral Ministry

Christian Friendship

Christian Friendship

The foundation of Christian soul care is its least specialized form—the friendship offered by one Christian to another.[2]

1. An expanded spectrum of forms of Christian soul care is described in *Care of Souls* (Benner 1998) from which some of this material on soul care is adapted.
2. A fuller discussion of Christian friendship can be found in *Sacred Companions* (Benner 2002).

Friends do not think of themselves as offering soul care when they call one another to offer support or encouragement or simply to maintain contact. They are simply caring for those they love. But friends who understand the high ideals of Christian companionship offer one of the most important forms of Christian soul care. And if we could more regularly be in relationships in which friends and family cared for us in our totality with particular attention to the inner self, the need for more formal and specialized expressions of soul care would be greatly reduced.

Christian friendship is both important and possible because it has its source in God. The Christian doctrine of the Trinity places friendship at the very heart of the nature of God. And almost unbelievably, the eternal exchange of companionship that binds Father, Son, and Holy Spirit to one another extends to those Jesus calls to be his followers and friends. It is this friendship that Jesus asks us to show to one another (1 John 4:7).

At its best, the care that family members and friends give to one another has the unique potential to encourage deep growth and healing. Parents, as they nurture the psychological and spiritual aspects of their children, have opportunities to influence their children in ways that no one else will ever have, as do couples who make a genuine effort to know and support the inner life of their spouse.

Unfortunately, families often fail to live up to the ideals of soul friendship. Parents content themselves with discipline and instruction, failing to offer themselves also in a gift of friendship. Tragically, of course, couples easily and regularly do the same. Too often those who are active in caring for others outside the home offer little genuine soul friendship to those within their own family.

Churches that seek to establish the mutual soul care offered between friends and family members as the foundation of the soul care provided by the congregation must start by helping families become networks of genuine soul friendship. They must both encourage and support friendships between nonfamily members that do not resemble mere generic fellowship but reflect nothing less than the ideals of mutual soul care.

17

Pastoral counseling is not friendship, nor can it be offered without hazard to someone with whom the pastor has a personal friendship.[3] But pastoral counseling can best fulfill its distinctive role when it is offered within a community that is based on a network of genuine soul-care friendships.

Pastoral Ministry

Pastoral ministry also forms part of the broad context of pastoral counseling. It includes such things as preaching, teaching, leading worship, administration, community service, leadership development, and, of course, pastoral care and counseling (Clinebell 1984). Although the boundaries among these spheres of responsibility are sometimes unclear, it is important that these diverse activities fit together as a whole. Thus, no one activity can be undertaken in a way that compromises others. This is particularly important in the case of pastoral care and counseling, which can easily consume time intended for other responsibilities and which can be entered into in a way that produces significant conflict with other aspects of the pastoral role. Pastoral counseling must, therefore, be conducted in a way that minimizes conflict with these other pastoral roles.

Preaching, teaching, and worship are all particularly vital soul-care activities. Anything that brings people into contact with God nurtures the growth of their spirits and heals their souls. This is why most pastors rightly understand worship as central to the life of a congregation. We can think of it as corporate soul care in that, at its best, it integrates and gives direction to all the other forms of soul care offered within a congregation.

Pastoral counseling must be offered in such a way as to support, never compromise, these broader responsibilities of pastoral ministry. Most pastors, except for those who do only counseling, must fit counseling within the range of other

3. See the discussion of ethical guidelines in the appendix for further perspective on this matter.

responsibilities that fill the week. This means it must fit not only within available and limited time (about which I will have more to say shortly) but also within the network of other roles the pastor fills.

One area of potential conflict is between counseling and preaching. Should sermons be drawn from one's counseling experiences? To do so, in a direct and obvious manner, violates the confidentiality of the counseling encounter. One must realize that respecting this all-important counseling norm of confidentiality requires more than protecting a person's name (Nessan 1998). Even if one has planned a sermon on homosexuality, for example, it is probably not a good idea to give it right after hearing about a parishioner's struggles in this area. Doing so would undoubtedly make the parishioner feel that the pastor was using the pulpit to say something to him or her specifically.

But on the other hand, to fail to allow one's preaching to be informed by one's counseling is to fail to utilize a rich source of information about one's congregation and to speak dynamically to their deepest needs. The answer to this dilemma lies, of course, in Spirit-guided discernment about when and how to address such issues. The pastor should also not overlook the simple option of discussing the sermon topic with the individual concerned. This is an easy way to show sensitivity and can be the ounce of prevention that saves the pound of remediation.

Pastoral Care

Pastoral ministry is broader than pastoral care; so too, pastoral care is broader than pastoral counseling. To attempt to reduce all pastoral care to counseling is to fail to recognize both the breadth of pastoral care as well as the distinctive nature of counseling.

As the term is commonly employed, pastoral care refers to the total range of help offered by pastors, elders, deacons, and other members of a congregation to those they seek to serve. Pastoral care is a ministry of compassion, and its source and motivation is the love of God. In its most basic form, pastoral care is simply a Christian reaching out with help, encouragement, or support to another at a time of need. Pastoral care is the gift of Christian love and nurture from one who attempts to mediate the gracious presence of God to another who desires, to one degree or another, to live life in the reality of that divine presence.

Eschmann (2000) suggests that pastoral care includes three broad types of activities: blessing and healing, reconciliation and conversion, and sanctification and fellowship. More specifically, it includes such things as visiting the sick, attending to the dying, comforting the bereaved, encouraging reconciliation of the estranged, supporting those who are struggling or facing difficulties of any kind, nurturing and protecting the faith of those within the congregation, preaching, teaching, intercessory prayer, and administering the sacraments.

Healthy congregations build on the foundation of friendships that form the core of spiritual community by encouraging all Christians to reach out to one another in relationships of pastoral care. Describing all acts of Christian care as "friendship," however, trivializes friendship. Friendships should be mutual, whereas acts of pastoral care should be offered with no expectation of anything in return. Congregations that include an ever increasing number of members and adherents who are concerned about the welfare of others within the fellowship are congregations that place soul care at the heart of ministry.

Pastoral counseling is also an activity of pastoral care, though it differs from these other pastoral-care activities in several important ways. First, whereas a relationship of pastoral care can appropriately be initiated by a pastor or someone else offering care, pastoral counseling is usually initiated by a parishioner. Furthermore, pastoral counseling typically has more of a problem focus; that is, a parishioner contacts the pastor because of something that is problematic and for which he or she seeks help. While pastoral care may be delivered in the face of difficult life experiences, these are usually seen not so much as problems that need to be solved as experiences that need to be understood theologically and faced with the awareness of the presence of God.

Pastoral-care activities also usually involve less time than is the case with pastoral counseling—even a brief form of counseling such as strategic pastoral counseling. Acts of marriage, burial, or visitation do not usually involve an ongoing relationship of pastoral care. Even marriage preparation (sometimes called premarital counseling but usually lacking the problem focus of other forms of counseling) is typically time-limited.

Furthermore, pastoral care does not require the same level of involvement or responsiveness that is necessary in pastoral counseling. It is quite appropriate, for example, to offer pastoral care to people who are unconscious (see, for example, Close 1998), nonverbal, or even profoundly mentally retarded—all conditions that would suggest limited usefulness for pastoral counseling.

Finally, whereas in other pastoral-care activities, biblical precepts are sometimes appropriately introduced immediately and directly, in pastoral counseling, sharing passages from the Bible is not appropriate until the pastor has heard the parishioner's story. Even then, Scripture should be shared as part of an ongoing dialogue. This process takes more time than is available in brief pastoral-care encounters in which a quick sharing of prayer or a verse of Scripture is sometimes appropriate if the parishioner desires it.

Spiritual Direction

Apart from Anglicans and Episcopalians, most Protestants, until recently, have been unfamiliar with the concept of spiritual direction. Those who have heard of it have often equated it with the notion of submission to a religious authority, perhaps thinking of it as something for monks or others in religious orders. Consequently, they have tended to view it with misgiving. Others, aware of the attention that spiritual direction has received recently, have viewed it simply as a fad, nothing more than the latest packaging of discipling or

21

mentoring. Still others, while realizing that spiritual direction is ancient rather than new, have assumed that it is something like spiritual counseling—that is, moral guidance or some other form of advice about how to put one's spiritual life in order.

All of these reactions are based on serious misunderstandings. Spiritual direction, the jewel in the crown of soul-care relationships, has been an important part of formal relationships of Christian nurture since the earliest days of the church. Rather than being for a specialized few, it is highly relevant to every Christian who takes the spiritual journey seriously. Rather than being a relationship of authority, it is a form of spiritual friendship. Rather than being focused on morality, its focus is one's relationship with God. And rather than being simply a context for dispensing spiritual advice, it is a relationship of co-discernment. The "director" acknowledges the Spirit as the true spiritual director and seeks to help the other discern and submit to the leading of the Spirit.

Spiritual direction is "a prayer process in which a person seeking help in cultivating a deeper personal relationship with God meets with another for prayer and conversation that is focused on increasing awareness of God in the midst of life experiences and facilitating surrender to God's will" (Benner 2002, 94). Let me unpack this definition by examining some of its component parts.

Regardless of whether eyes are closed or words are spoken, prayer is foundational to spiritual direction because—at its core—spiritual direction involves both the director and the directee seeking to be attentive to the presence of God and to respond to that awareness. Spiritual direction involves a set of relationships between three persons—the director, the directee, and God. Central to this is not the relationship between the director and the directee but the relationship between the directee and God. This is different from counseling, in which the relationship between the counselor and the counselee is of primary importance. Spiritual directors must avoid overvaluing their relationship with those they seek to help. The relationship of primary importance is the relationship between the one seeking spiritual direction and the Lord, and the overall goal is helping the directee attend to the leading and the presence of the Spirit in his or her life and surrender to God's love and will.

While pastoral counseling and spiritual direction share some common features, they differ in important ways. The most important of these differences is that while counseling is problem centered, spiritual direction is Spirit centered. Although spiritual direction could theoretically be initiated by a crisis or a problem, its goal is growth in one's relationship with God, not resolution of a problem. The problem, if there is one, is merely the place where one can expect to meet God.

Another important difference between pastoral counseling and spiritual direction is seen in the role of empathy in the relationship. Counselors seek to be empathic to the inner experience of those they counsel. Spiritual directors, on the other hand, make their empathic focus not the other person but the Holy Spirit. This means that the spiritual director's goal is not primarily to understand how the person seeking direction feels, nor is it to enter the person's experience and see the world as he or she sees it. Rather, the goal is to help the person more closely encounter the Spirit of God.

Shea (1997) suggests that while both pastoral counseling and spiritual direction share a focus on faith development, they differ in their approach. Pastoral counseling seeks to help people reach mature faith, while spiritual direction seeks to help those with mature faith deepen such faith by living it out in the midst of life. Galindo (1997) adds to this by suggesting that spiritual direction focuses on the way in which grace operates in the life of the person seeking help—how it is accepted, resisted, and responded to in prayer and action.

Pastoral counselors can learn much from this often neglected expression of Christian soul care. Attentiveness to the presence and leading of the Spirit anchors pastoral counseling in Christian soul care and helps a pastor not to take responsibility for the growth or healing of the one seeking help. The role of silence in the process—as both participants seek to heighten their attentiveness to the Spirit—is also relevant to the pastoral counseling process. But perhaps no contribution is more important than the understanding of the role of the

Spirit as the true director. Pastoral counselors do well to recall that the same Spirit is also the true counselor. The role of the pastoral counselor is to aid attunement and surrender to this truly wonderful Counselor, the one to whom both parties in the process should be looking.

Some congregations are fortunate enough to have trained spiritual directors on staff or within the congregation. Others have to rely on the pastor or other mature Christians who make themselves available to accompany those who seek relationships of spiritual accountability and growth. No one need be without the accompaniment of a spiritual director as long as wise and mature Christians are willing to learn how to come alongside others as they seek to be aware of God's presence and leading. No Christian should be without a spiritual director, and no congregation should fail to encourage the development of those whom God has gifted for this calling.

Pastoral Counseling

Counseling that is done by pastors must fit within this context of soul-care ministries. This means that it will differ in important ways from generic Christian counseling, that is, counseling offered by Christians who are not explicitly identified with a pastoral role. Non-pastoral Christian counseling may be shaped by Christian values and built around a Christian view of persons, but seldom does it have the explicit spiritual focus that is appropriate in pastoral counseling. Furthermore, because its practitioners are mental-health professionals rather than clergy, Christian counseling builds on a clinical relationship that is quite different from the pastoral relationship that should be at the core of pastoral counseling.

Pastoral counseling is different from Christian counseling because the pastor is much more than a counselor. Pastors relate to those they counsel in a variety of ways, each reflecting one facet of the broad spectrum of pastoral responsibilities. Unlike the clinical counselor, whether Christian or non-Christian, the pastoral counselor does not have the option of restricting contact with those seen in counseling to the scheduled counseling sessions. The pastor who counsels also engages with parishioners from the pulpit, in committees, at congregational fellowship events, and at the door after church on Sunday mornings. The pastor also visits parishioners when they are sick and marries and buries them. These activities are all integral aspects of the pastoral role, and counseling must be undertaken in a way that supports these other equally important pastoral relationships.

But just as pastoral counseling is located within the broad range of pastoral ministries, so too it must be positioned within the field of counseling. Whatever else it is, pastoral counseling is a form of counseling; therefore, we must understand its relationship to other activities that are described by this same word.

The term *counseling* is used, of course, in diverse ways, with advice about taxes, travel, nutrition, and many other matters all being called counseling. When used to describe such activities, counseling refers to information exchange or the giving of advice. In contrast to this, mental-health professionals use the word to refer to a helping relationship in which, through a series of structured contacts, a counselor seeks to alleviate distress and promote growth in the one seeking help. In this case, counseling describes a relationship of dialogue and exploration, not simply one of information exchange.

These two understandings of counseling are not mutually exclusive but are, rather, on a continuum. The giving of advice may be a part of the counseling of a mental-health professional, although it is seldom the major part. Similarly, a tax counselor may take personal interest in the one seeking advice and may respond with empathy, not merely technical advice. However, this is not the essence of such counseling. We really have no right to expect such a relationship with a tax consultant. And in the same way, we should expect more than advice from a mental-health professional.

Where, then, does pastoral counseling fall on this continuum of counseling as advice to counseling as a helping relationship designed to alleviate distress and promote growth? Although there are many ways in which pastoral counseling may be legitimately offered, in general it is closer to psychological counseling than to tax counseling. This may appear to be nothing more than another accommodation to the psychological sciences. However, the history of Christian soul care supports this positioning of pastoral counseling as more than simple advice giving. While spiritual guidance sometimes involves the act of giving advice, the overall emphasis is clearly on the formation of a relationship between one who is spiritually mature and one who is seeking spiritual help, and this relationship is designed to aid the spiritual growth of the one seeking help (McNeil 1951; Clebsch and Jaekle 1964). Typical of this understanding is the seventeenth-century French theologian Fénelon, who offers the following timeless advice on the conduct of pastoral counsel:

> Speak little; listen much; think far more of understanding hearts and of adapting yourself to their needs than of saying clever things to them. Show that you have an open mind, and let every one see by experience that there is safety and consolation in opening his mind to you. Avoid extreme severity, and reprove, where necessary, with caution and gentleness. Never say more than is needed, but let whatever you say be said with entire frankness. Let no one fear to be deceived by trusting you. . . . You should become all things to all the children of God, for the sake of gaining every one of them. And correct yourself, for the sake of correcting others. (Fénelon 1980, 24)

Counseling, whether conducted by a pastor or a mental-health professional, is not reducible, therefore, to telling a person what to do or what not to do, whether it be the counselor's opinion or the counselor's opinion of God's opinion. While pastoral counseling must always be offered in the light of God's Word—which is expected of a representative of the Christian church—pastoral counseling is not the same as preaching or any of the other pastoral responsibilities.

One way of understanding the essence of counseling is to think of it as a structured way of being with a person who seeks help. Counseling is first and foremost about being, not doing—not so much about the skillful application of techniques as about being a certain kind of person and bringing that self to counseling in a helpful manner. Carl Jung is reputed to have said that it is not what you do or what you know that makes the difference in counseling but rather who you are. The psychospiritual well-being of the pastoral counselor does more to enhance or limit the helpfulness of counseling than any other single factor associated with either the counselor or the counseling process. It is difficult to lead others to places where one has never been. Therefore, the counselor who does not exemplify, even to an imperfect extent, the priorities and principles that lie behind his or her counseling will be seriously limited in helping others.

But counseling is not merely being; it is being with. If counseling begins with the person of the counselor, it quickly moves beyond this to the way of being as a person with another person. Olthius (1989) suggests that being-with is the basic metaphor of the Christian faith, that which best captures the essence of the covenant relationship that God offers his people. Just as God offers his people his faithful presence in the midst of their suffering, brokenness, and struggles, so too a counselor can offer to be with those who seek his or her help. Being with others in their struggles existentially captures the heart of what counseling is all about. In this special way, a counselor is able to demonstrate compassion and to offer an incarnate form of care as he or she comes to the one who suffers and shares that suffering.

Finally, counseling is a structured being-with. This means that it is, to some extent at least, rule bound. Not all ways of being with a person are equally effective in mediating grace and bringing that person into direct personal contact with God. This is the goal of pastoral counseling, and the structures, disciplines, and techniques involved in the relationship should all ultimately serve this purpose. Counseling involves a disciplined form of being-with, and this discipline is shaped by the theory and techniques of one's approach to counseling. These guide and direct the counseling, helping to set the priorities and to determine, secure, and maintain the desired focus.

Pastoral counseling is both a specialized form of pastoral care and a specialized form of counseling. It should be set apart from other pastoral contacts by means of specific appointments that are held in a consistent and appropriate setting. Pastoral counseling is not appropriately done in hallways, doorways, or in the narthex before a worship service. Not all pastor-parishioner conversations regarding parishioner concerns are pastoral counseling. Pastoral counseling, as any specialized relationship, requires boundaries that protect its special purposes. These boundaries are essential if it is to be appropriately set apart from other responsibilities of pastoral care and ministry.

If pastoral counseling is to be distinctively and authentically pastoral, it must be returned to its proper place within pastoral care and ministry. It must also be understood in relationship to the other forms of Christian soul care that form a part of the life of the church. Each of the forms of soul care fills a unique part of the spectrum, and each can function best when supported by the presence of the others.

Additional Readings

Aden, L., and J. H. Ellens, eds. 1988. *The church and pastoral care.* Grand Rapids: Baker. A collection of articles on the role of pastoral care in the church that presents a thorough and balanced overview of all aspects of pastoral care.

Benner, D. 1998. *The care of souls: Revisioning Christian nurture and counsel.* Grand Rapids: Baker. After offering a brief review of the history of Christian soul care, this book explores the ways in which the psychological and spiritual aspects of such care can be combined in a broad spectrum of contemporary forms of Christian care, nurture, and counsel.

———. 2002. *Sacred companions: The gift of spiritual friendship and direction.* Downers Grove, Ill.: InterVarsity. This book provides a helpful introduction to spiritual direction, positioning it as a specialized form of the more general relationship of spiritual friendship, and includes extended discussion of its relationship to counseling.

Gerkin, C. V. 1997. *An introduction to pastoral care.* Nashville: Abingdon. An excellent overview of historic and contemporary pastoral-care practices from an author with more than fifty years of experience in the clinical pastoral education movement.

Holifield, E. B. 1983. *A history of pastoral care in America*. Nashville: Abingdon. A scholarly treatment of the modern history of pastoral care for the person interested in something substantial yet easily readable.

McNeil, J. 1951. *A history of the cure of souls*. New York: Harper & Row. This is probably the definitive history of the care and cure of souls in Christianity. Its relevance to the present chapter lies in its clear demonstration of the central place such soul care played in church history.

Nessan, C. 1998. Confidentiality: Sacred trust and ethical quagmire. *Journal of Pastoral Care* 52, no. 4:349–57. Contains a particularly helpful discussion of the ethics and practicalities of pastoral confidentiality.

Pattison, S. 1988. *A critique of pastoral care*. London: SCM. Much more than a critique, this is a balanced and carefully researched overview of the ministry of pastoral care. It provides a particularly useful treatment of the role of the Bible in the development of pastoral theology and the practice of pastoral care.

Ruffing, J. 2000. *Spiritual direction: Beyond the beginnings*. New York: Paulist Press. An excellent resource for the pastoral counselor who already knows something about spiritual direction and wants to go beyond the basics.

Wiersbe, D. W. 2000. *The dynamics of pastoral care*. Grand Rapids: Baker. A basic but helpful discussion of some of the principal forms of congregational-based pastoral care.

2

The Uniqueness of Pastoral Counseling

Although pastoral counseling shares features with counseling done by other professionals, it has a number of important distinctives. Table 1 summarizes five of them.

Table 1

The Uniqueness of Pastoral Counseling

The training of the pastoral counselor
The role of the pastoral counselor
The context of pastoral counseling
The goals of pastoral counseling
The resources of pastoral counseling

The Training of the Pastoral Counselor

The training of ministers is distinctive because it provides pastoral counselors with a spiritual perspective on persons and their problems. Ministers are the only counseling professionals who routinely have training in systematic theology, biblical studies, ethics, and church history, and this framework of understanding gives pastoral counselors an invaluable perspective on those seeking their help. What a shame, therefore, when ministers abandon this perspective for a psychological one, judging the latter to be superior or more prestigious. Christian psychotherapists may, with the help of theological reading and reflection, bring their understanding of persons into line with a Christian view, but the clinical filters through which they see people make their perspective different from that of pastors. The training of pastors provides them with a unique and vitally important perspective. It equips them to see people spiritually, that is, in the light of their relationship with God and their response to this relationship.

Properly understood, a spiritual perspective should always be a holistic perspective. Apart from immature and unhealthy forms of spirituality that limit our experience of God to one sphere of our being, the human encounter with the divine always has ripple effects that spread out to touch all aspects of our being. Christian soul care should always involve a focus on the whole person, with particular attention given to the inner self. Pastoral counselors are in a unique position to provide this, for their training offers them the opportunity to understand people from the biggest of all perspectives—the spiritual.

Training that is strong in one area will, by necessity, be weaker in others. When compared to psychologists, psychiatrists, and psychotherapists, pastoral counselors typically have a more limited background in psychopathology, assessment and diagnosis, and psychotherapy. While pastors may have taken a course or two in pastoral psychology or counseling and possibly an internship or supervised experience in clinical pastoral education, their typical exposure to psychology is somewhat limited. Without advanced specialized training in psychotherapy, they should not, therefore, attempt long-term approaches to counseling that seek to change underlying personality structures or resolve deep-seated unconscious problems and conflicts.

Ministers are uniquely equipped to foster spiritual whole-ness, and this should be the heart of any counseling that is called pastoral. This spiritual focus builds on the distinctive strengths of pastoral training and represents an approach to counseling that is not only consonant with other aspects of the pastoral role but also allows counseling to be integrated into the context of pastoral care and ministry.

The Role of the Pastoral Counselor

Pastors are also unique among counselors because of their social and symbolic roles. They are religious authority figures and, like it or not, symbolically represent religious values and beliefs. People approach pastors, therefore, with different expectations than those associated with other helping profes-sionals. They expect pastors to represent Christian values, beliefs, and commitments and to "bring Christian meaning to bear on human problems" (Clebsch and Jaekle 1964, 4–5).

Because ministers are perceived as representatives of the Christian church, some people avoid approaching them when struggling with personal problems. The reasons for this are quite varied and are associated with idiosyncratic responses to the symbolic role of clergy. Many adults continue to see clergy through the eyes of their childhood, possibly recalling judgmental or punitive encounters with strict and intimidat-ing religious authority figures. It is understandable that such people are afraid of approaching a pastoral counselor at a time of need. Others have more positive associations with clergy but, assuming them to be interested in only explicitly religious matters, judge their own problems as too mundane or secular for a religious professional.

But these same associations and expectations cause a majority of people to come to the opposite conclusion. In an important and now quite well-known study conducted in 1957, 42 percent of Americans reported that when facing a significant personal problem, a minister is the first person they would consult when seeking help. A family physician was preferred by 29 percent of the sample (Gurin, Verhoff, and

33

Feld 1960). When this study was replicated in 1976, ministers were still the most preferred group of helpers, chosen by 39 percent of the people (Verhoff, Kukla, and Dorran 1981). The second most popular professional group at this time was psychologists and psychiatrists, who were chosen by 29 percent of the sample. Nonpsychiatric physicians dropped to third place, being the first choice of 21 percent of the people.

These statistics demonstrate that in spite of what often seems to be a diminishing sphere of influence for the church in society, a considerably higher percentage of people go to the clergy for help with personal problems than to any other helping profession. And they make this choice because of the clergy's role as representatives of the Christian church who bring both a Christian perspective and unique Christian healing resources to their work as counselors.

The Context of Pastoral Counseling

Closely related to the role expectations associated with being a minister of the Christian church are the symbolic associations related to the context of pastoral counseling, that is, the church. Hiltner and Colston studied the process of counseling in different contexts and discovered that, other things being equal, counseling proceeded faster in a church context (Hiltner and Colston 1961). They concluded that the reason for this was that the symbols and expectations associated with the church made it immediately clear where the pastoral counselor stood on important value matters. The counselee, therefore, needed less time to get to know the counselor's values. Other common associations related to the church, such as it being a place of quiet or safety or where one meets God, also serve to facilitate the counseling conducted within a church context.

But of even more value is the fact that the church is not merely a building but a community of faith. Ideally, a minister counsels within a setting of established, trusting, caring relationships, and no other helping profession has a comparable community resource. If a congregation is, in fact, this sort of community, the pastor can connect people who are hurting with individuals and groups within the church who can provide love and support. Pastors should never feel that they are responsible for meeting all the needs of those who seek their help. Instead, they should see themselves in the role of a broker—bringing those who consult them into contact with the healing resources of the body and life of Christ. Seldom is the healing potential of this kind of fellowship fully realized. But as a congregation moves toward the ideal of being a community of spiritual friendships, a pastor can develop a unique and invaluable resource.

One final distinctive of the context of pastoral counseling relates to the ongoing nature of contacts between pastor and parishioners. As noted earlier, pastors counsel within a network of relationships in which people know and see one another in a variety of situations. This enhances trust and thus greatly facilitates the counseling process. It also means that ministers are often able to identify problems before they reach advanced stages and have the opportunity of early intervention. Psychotherapists often see people much too late. Furthermore, they are not in a position to take the initiative in reaching out to someone needing help.

The Goals of Pastoral Counseling

A clear understanding of the goals of counseling is one of the most important aspects of any counseling relationship. Without clear goals, counseling becomes an aimless activity in which the means become the end. Furthermore, the goals of counseling are more determinative of the character of counseling than any other aspect, even more so than the techniques employed. If pastoral counseling is to be unique, its goals must be both clear and distinctive.

The main goal of pastoral counseling is the facilitation of spiritual growth. Like other counselors, pastors seek to provide whatever help is possible for the problems that are presented to them. But solving these problems is not their primary objective. Rather, their goal is to help people understand their problems—and their lives—in the light of their relationship with God and then to live more fully in the light of this understanding. In so doing, the pastoral counselor works toward the alleviation of problems because, as St. Irenius reminds us, the glory of God is men and women who are fully alive. But problems should never be the primary focus. The focus should be the whole person as he or she lives out life before the face of God.

The pastor's working premise is that spiritual growth is both foundational to all human wholeness and related to all other aspects of wholeness. There is no sphere of life that is not included within the spiritual. There is, therefore, no sphere of life that is irrelevant to pastoral counseling. Whether the focus is on grief in the face of bereavement, conflicts in a relationship, matters of vocational direction, struggles in prayer, addictions, or anxiety in the face of illness or impending death, the challenge is to assist the one seeking help to bring theological reflection to life experiences as a way of aiding spiritual growth.

To suggest that pastoral counselors have a primary concern for the facilitation of spiritual growth does not mean that they are concerned only, or even principally, with problems that appear to be spiritual. All problems have spiritual components because all of life is religious or spiritual. Furthermore, spiritual concerns emerge most clearly within the context of daily life experiences and struggles, and these are the natural focus of any counseling relationship. The uniqueness of pastoral counseling lies not in the problems it addresses but in its goal.

To bring this spiritual focus to bear on the problem being discussed requires great skill on a minister's part. The spiritual significance of a particular problem or experience must first be discerned and then gently identified. This requires that the pastor as counselor be sensitive to the Holy Spirit, who is the true counselor. Pastoral counselors should be keenly aware of their dependence on the Spirit, even as they are aware that healing comes not from the skillful application of techniques, nor from life itself, but from God, who is present in the midst of life and available as the source of all growth and constructive change.

The Resources of Pastoral Counseling

Finally, pastoral counseling is unique in its use of religious resources. Prayer, Scripture, the sacraments, anointing with oil, the laying on of hands, and devotional or religious literature are all (depending on one's religious tradition) potential resources for the counseling process. The failure to employ any of them suggests an erosion of the distinctively pastoral aspects of one's counseling.

We should note, however, that first and foremost these religious resources are for a pastoral counselor's own life. Only if they are used meaningfully in the personal life of the pastor can they be employed appropriately in counseling.

There is a high personal cost associated with the provision of counseling. Counseling a person who is confused, hurting, angry, or fearful necessarily involves absorbing significant amounts of that person's distress. I have elsewhere suggested that this absorption of the suffering and disease of the one seeking help mirrors in an imperfect way God's healing response to us in our sin (Benner 1983). While the pastoral counselor's actions do not have the ultimate salvatory effect that is present in Jesus' absorption of our sin, they do represent an essential component of the healing process.

The personal costs of counseling also remind us why it is so necessary for a counselor to experience continuous renewal through Scripture, prayer, and the sacraments. Only when one's own spiritual batteries are being continuously recharged can one hope to have something to give to others. And only in one's own personal walk with the Lord can one find the strength to bear not only one's own burdens but also those of others.

When these religious resources are used in counseling, it is crucial that they be employed with care and sensitivity. In particular, it is important that a pastor understand how they are experienced by the person seeking help. Prayer, Scripture reading, and other religious resources carry heavy, negative emotional freight for some people. They can also easily be used in ways that arouse inappropriate guilt or unnecessary discomfort or block creative dialogue.

For example, someone who goes to a pastor expecting conversation might experience prayer as an avoidance of such direct engagement. Similarly, reading Scripture can be seen as a way of hiding behind divine authority. Religious language and practices provide pastors with a readily available means of escaping the demands of serious dialogue, and retreating into the religious authority role can be a way of attempting to retain control of an uncomfortable or threatening situation (Hulme 1981). Genuine dialogue requires the relinquishment of control and the risk of an unpredictable outcome. But genuine dialogue allows us to move outside ourselves and to meet the other. And if the other is a pastoral counselor who is in touch with the Holy Other, the meeting has the potential of being genuinely transformational.

It is important, therefore, for pastors to know why a particular religious resource is being employed in any given situation. Is it a way of avoiding talking about an uncomfortable subject? Or might it be a way of providing premature reassurance, possibly even a way of relieving one's own anxiety or distress? To answer such questions, pastors must know themselves and be able to reflect on their behavior with a degree of objectivity and honesty. Without this self-scrutiny, pastoral counseling will seldom be more than a ritualistic exchange of clichés.

The appropriate use of religious resources in counseling is preceded by a pastor's awareness of both the person's problems as well as his or her religious background and present attitudes toward religion. This means that an assessment is necessary. Also, before using such resources, a pastor should ask whether they would be meaningful or appreciated. This demonstrates respect for the person's feelings and beliefs and will often open up profitable discussion about spiritual conflicts and blocks. And, of course, even if the person prefers that prayer or Scripture not be utilized in the session, this in no way limits prayer for the person at other times.

Clinebell notes that religious resources should always be used in ways that empower the person, never in ways that might diminish his or her sense of initiative, strength, or responsibility (Clinebell 1984, 123). This is particularly important with individuals who tend to be dependent and who easily rely on the "magic" of the pastor's prayers or Scripture reading rather than on learning to use such resources themselves. With such people, it is often appropriate for the pastor to ask them to pray rather than or in addition to simply praying for them.

Clinebell also suggests that a pastor should use such resources in ways that "facilitate rather than block the owning and catharsis of negative feelings" (123). This can be done, for example, through encouraging meditation on passages such as Psalm 6:6 ("I am worn out with groaning"), Psalm 13:1–2 ("How much longer will you forget me? . . . How much longer must I endure grief?"), Psalm 31:10 ("My life is worn out with sorrow"), Psalm 63:9–10 ("May those now hounding me to death go down to the earth below, consigned to the edge of the sword, and left as food for jackals"), Psalm 73:13–14 ("Why should I keep my own heart pure . . . if you plague me all day long?"), Psalm 109:8, 10, 14 ("Let his life be cut short. . . . May his children be homeless vagabonds. . . . May the crimes of his fathers be held against him and his mother's sin never be effaced"). These, and a large number of other biblical passages, make clear that God is no stranger to the expression of strong, raw emotions from his people and that he invites them to come to him in the midst of their confusion, doubt, rage, despair, and grief.

The essence of these religious resources is the dynamic contact they can provide between God and the one seeking pastoral help. Their use must never, therefore, be mechanical, legalistic, or magical. When used with sensitivity, however, they can uniquely help the person sense the caring, healing, and sustaining presence of a personal God. If they enhance this personal contact with God, they make an indispensable contribution to the counseling process. If they do not work to provide this contact, they are probably being misused.

Pastoral Counseling Defined

Having reviewed the distinctives of pastoral counseling, it is now time to attempt a more formal definition. *Pastoral counseling involves the establishment of a time-limited relationship that is structured to provide comfort for troubled persons by enhancing their awareness of God's grace and faithful presence and thereby increasing their ability to live their lives more fully in the light of these realizations.*

The essence of pastoral counseling is helping troubled people bring their woundedness, struggles, doubts, and anxieties into dynamic healing contact with the God who is known by his people as the wonderful Counselor. This is the most important thing a pastor can do. Anything that facilitates this direct, dynamic contact with God should be welcomed as a legitimate part of pastoral counseling, while anything that hinders it should be avoided. The help that pastors provide is not primarily related to their ability to produce sophisticated formulations of the nature of the problem or to their skillful implementation of counseling techniques and interventions. Rather, it is primarily a result of their ability to mediate God's presence to the people who consult them. Through their words and their being, they should move people toward a closer contact with the God who heals, sustains, guides, reconciles, and nurtures his people.

The special relationship known as pastoral counseling is a time-limited relationship. It is not the ongoing relationship of pastoral care that a pastor has with all the parishioners. Rather, it is set up in response to a request for help, structured in ways to facilitate its purposes, and terminated when these purposes have been accomplished. Other pastoral-care responsibilities are usually not terminated at any time other than at a person's death or departure from the church or community. Pastoral counseling is, by its very nature, a special and unique relationship. Like emergency room care, it is a form of intensive treatment that should be replaced as soon as possible by more regular and ongoing care, in this case, pastoral care.

Pastoral counseling is related to other forms of counseling in its use of a structured relationship for the amelioration of distress and the facilitation of growth. Pastoral counselors seek to help people who have problems and who consult them. In this way, they are like other counselors. However, the way in which they provide help is unique. They help by representing Christian values and understandings and by bringing people into contact with a source of help and healing that exists outside the counselors themselves. In this regard, pastoral counselors always see God as a partner in the counseling process, and this partnership should provide considerable relief of the pressures that accompany the bearing of burdens of troubled persons.

The training, role, context, goals, and resources of pastoral counseling combine to give the pastoral counselor a number of advantages over other counseling professionals. Table 2 summarizes several of these.

Table 2

Advantages of the Pastoral Counselor

The ability to bring theological reflection to bear on life experiences
The holistic perspective that accompanies the spiritual focus
The availability of religious and congregational resources
The facilitation of trust associated with knowledge of a pastor's values and worldview
The ability to relate in ways that are not restricted to the counseling role
The ability to provide services regardless of capacity to pay[1]

The Case for Brief Pastoral Counseling

When the first edition of this book was published in 1992, there was only one other model of short-term pastoral coun-

1. Although the typical absence of a fee for counseling provided by parish pastors is in general an advantage, the absence of a fee sometimes decreases a person's commitment to the process. A helpful discussion of the complex clinical issues associated with fees in counseling is provided by Danco (1982) and Benner (1999). Campbell's (1985) discussion of the professionalization of pastoral counseling is also noteworthy.

seling (Childs 1990). Pastoral counseling—like counseling in general—was primarily a long-term undertaking. Brief counseling was thought to be superficial, the presumption being that it failed to get at the root of a problem and treated only symptoms. Therefore, it was assumed that apart from providing support for people going through crises, brief approaches provided little real help. It was also generally assumed that any modest changes associated with short-term counseling would be of limited durability.

Given these biases, it is not surprising that most people considered brief counseling inferior to long-term counseling. Nor is it surprising that pastoral counselors—wanting to avoid being seen as inferior and superficial—gravitated toward traditional long-term approaches.

This began to change with the rise of managed health care. Counselors and psychotherapists suddenly faced pressure to shorten the duration of counseling. Though resisting such changes, counselors were surprised to discover just how effective brief counseling often was. In fact, counselors quickly discovered that rather than simply being a poor substitute for long-term counseling, short-term counseling was often equally effective. Several decades of research have provided ample confirmation of this initial finding (Lambert and Bergin 1994).

But the case for short-term pastoral counseling is even stronger. For parish pastors who counsel, available time, role diversity, and typical background in psychology are often strong reasons for pastors to adopt a brief counseling approach.

No pastor I have ever known has had the time to see everyone within his or her congregation who was in need of counseling. Even pastors whose primary responsibility is care and counseling find their time in short supply. The press of other responsibilities usually makes it possible to see only people in acute crisis. This is unfortunate because it undermines the unique pastoral advantage of possible early intervention and prevention-oriented counseling. However, as any pastor knows, the demands of ministry are a constant pressure, limiting the time available for counseling. Clearly, a brief counseling approach simply fits the time available.

A second feature of the pastoral situation that supports a short-term approach to counseling is the diversity of roles played by a parish pastor. We have already noted that the fact that pastoral counselors often relate to those they counsel in other roles is an advantage. Many parishioners prefer to see their pastor when they need counseling precisely because he or she is already a part of their network of relationships.

But there are also potential complications associated with this switching of hats, especially when pastors see those they counsel in other contexts and roles. Both may feel uncomfortable when encountering each other at a church dinner the evening after a particularly difficult counseling session. Or the person seeking counseling may be unsure how to respond to a social greeting and question about how he is doing when meeting the pastor at the door after a sermon. Eliminating these complications is the reason psychotherapists attempt to limit all extra-therapeutic contacts and generally refuse to counsel those with whom they have some other relationship or involvement. Pastors who counsel obviously cannot do this. But one way in which they can minimize the role conflicts they often encounter is by keeping counseling relationships short-term.

Finally, as noted earlier, the psychological training of most pastors has important implications for the sort of counseling they should undertake. Some models of pastoral counseling presuppose an advanced knowledge of personality and psychotherapy theory and are of limited usefulness for pastors who have taken only one or two courses in pastoral psychology or counseling.[2] Most pastors simply do not have the necessary background to provide intensive psychotherapy or to provide complete treatment for severely disturbed individuals. Pastors, like all other professional counselors, must, therefore, be clearly aware of their limits of competence and ready and willing to make referrals once these limits are reached. Pastoral counseling should not be seen as a replacement for

2. Childs's work (1990) is a good example of such a model. It is an adaptation of psychoanalytic psychotherapy that requires a level of clinical skill and theoretical sophistication that would normally be associated with only advanced training in pastoral counseling or clinical pastoral education.

other medical and psychological therapies. Yet at the same time, much can be done within the limits of pastoral counseling. Even when other therapies are required, pastoral counseling is still a distinctive and valuable supplement to the total care. In short, there is no one for whom pastoral counseling is inappropriate. There are only people for whom it may be insufficient by itself.

On the basis of these considerations, it seems that pastoral counseling is best positioned as brief counseling. Long-term, intensive therapy is not a good use of the limited time of most pastors, nor do most pastors possess the necessary training for this type of therapy. Short-term counseling also allows a pastor to avoid the most intense transference reactions that may accompany long-term counseling relationships. Finally, short-term counseling is more appropriate for pastors who have many pastoral ministry responsibilities.

A number of approaches to short-term pastoral counseling have been proposed since the first edition of this book. Stone, the developer of one such approach (Stone 1994) and the editor of an excellent overview of ten others (Stone 2001), recently noted that the most important feature these diverse approaches share is the desire to "get people moving in a positive direction of their own choosing and then get out of the way" (Stone 1999, 43). All require that the pastor abandon grandiose goals—such as changing personality or resolving all of a person's problems—and understand the value of small changes that will break inertia and initiate movement in a positive direction. And all are highly focused on whatever is considered to be the master goal of the process and are structured to ensure that successive sessions steadily move toward this goal. Strategic pastoral counseling was designed to do precisely these things, and we turn now to the ways in which it does them.

Additional Readings

Browning, D. 1976. *The moral context of pastoral care.* Philadelphia: Westminster. Defining pastoral care as a "method of moral inquiry," this classic treatment of the role of moral considerations in pastoral care and counseling is well deserving of its continuing popularity.

Campbell, A. 1985. *Professionalism and pastoral care.* Philadelphia: Fortress. A thought-provoking consideration of the limits and dangers of professionalism in ministry.

Clebsch, W., and C. Jaekle. 1964. *Pastoral care in historical perspective.* Englewood Cliffs, N.J.: Prentice-Hall. An excellent overview of the history of pastoral care that is particularly useful in understanding the role of the pastoral counselor.

Clinebell, H. 1984. *Basic types of pastoral care and counseling.* Nashville: Abingdon. A good general overview of all aspects of pastoral counseling that clearly sets forth its uniqueness.

Doehring, C. 1995. *Taking care: Monitoring power dynamics and relational boundaries in pastoral care and counseling.* Nashville: Abingdon. This book offers a helpful discussion of the dynamics of power in pastoral counseling and care—helpful for any pastoral counselor, essential for those who are not sure what the issue is.

Hulme, W. 1981. *Pastoral care and counseling.* Minneapolis: Augsburg. Presents a good discussion of the unique Christian resources that are available to the pastoral counselor.

Oates, W. 1962. *Protestant pastoral counseling.* Philadelphia: Westminster. A good overview of all aspects of pastoral counseling that contains a particularly helpful treatment of the role and goals of the pastoral counselor.

Stone, H., ed. 2001. *Strategies for brief pastoral counseling.* Minneapolis: Fortress. An excellent overview of eleven contemporary approaches to brief pastoral counseling, all sharing a distinctive pastoral and parish emphasis.

Wimberly, D. 1990. *Prayer in pastoral counseling.* Louisville: Westminster/John Knox. An excellent discussion of the ways in which prayer can be used in counseling, not merely as a technique but rather as the very heart of the process.

3

The Strategic Pastoral
Counseling Model

Strategic pastoral counseling is a brief, structured counseling approach that is explicitly Christian and that appropriates the insights of contemporary counseling theory without sacrificing the resources of pastoral ministry. The term *strategic* emphasizes the fact that this approach to counseling is highly focused and time-limited. The term *pastoral* points to the fact that it is offered by a representative of the Christian church who is accountable to the church. The term *counseling* means that the help offered is organized around the problems experienced by those seeking pastoral assistance.

Seven characteristics of this model are particularly important. Strategic pastoral counseling is brief and time-limited, holistic, structured, involves assigned work between sessions, and is church-based, spiritually focused, and explicitly Christian. These are summarized in table 3 and will be discussed in order.

Table 3
Characteristics of Strategic Pastoral Counseling

Brief and time-limited
Holistic
Structured
Involves assigned homework
Church-based
Spiritually focused
Explicitly Christian

Brief and Time-Limited Counseling

Counseling can be brief (that is, conducted in relatively few sessions), or time-limited (that is, conducted within an initially fixed number of total sessions), or both. Strategic pastoral counseling is both brief and time-limited, working within a suggested maximum of five sessions.

Time-limited counseling incorporates all the advantages of brief counseling while adding some of its own. Here, both counselor and client are aware from the beginning of the total number of sessions. The clock is ticking from the first contact, and both the pastor and the parishioner are forced to work continuously at maintaining focus and direction. Contemporary versions of time-limited counseling usually set the total number of sessions somewhere in the ten- to fifteen-session range. However, this is more than is needed for the bulk of the counseling done by pastors. Background research conducted for the first edition of this book indicated that 87 percent of the pastoral counseling conducted by pastors in general ministry involves five or fewer sessions. The suggested maximum number of sessions for strategic pastoral counseling, therefore, is five.

All brief, time-limited approaches to counseling share four common principles, presented in table 4. These also serve as defining principles for strategic pastoral counseling.

Table 4
Principles of Brief, Time-Limited Counseling
The counselor must be active and directive
The counseling relationship must be a partnership
The counseling must concentrate on one central and specific problem
Time limitation must be maintained

The Strategic Pastoral Counselor Must Be Active and Directive

Strategic pastoral counseling requires that the pastoral counselor be both active and directive. While the nondirective counseling approach of Carl Rogers (1961) has made important contributions to pastoral counseling by stressing the importance and demands of listening, the somewhat passive posture associated with this tradition does not serve strategic pastoral counselors well. The counselor in any brief, time-limited approach is responsible for directing both the content and the process of the session. Typically, over the course of any given session, the strategic pastoral counselor will have as much to say as the parishioner. In contrast, in long-term counseling, it is common for the counselor to have substantially less to say than the one receiving the counseling. A failure to take this active direction-giving posture is a failure to provide the first and most basic ingredient of strategic pastoral counseling.

As we will see later, this more active posture can never be at the expense of careful listening. That which makes strategic pastoral counseling counseling as opposed to preaching is precisely the fact that it involves a dialogue, not a monologue. Good dialogue always requires careful, attentive listening. Therapeutic dialogue makes such listening foundational. This sort of attentive, empathic listening is not in any way incompatible with the active style of counseling that is the hallmark of strategic pastoral counseling.

Listen in on a portion of a second session to get a sense of this quality of active and directive listening. Rudy has been telling his pastor about his crisis of faith, which is the central problem they have agreed would be their focus. However, his relationship with God and his relationship with people keep getting intertwined. This is what Rudy is talking about at this point in the session.

Rudy: I find I am much less interested in answers than questions. It really bothers me that when I express my questions, most people in the church simply hear an invitation to offer pet clichés as potential answers. No one really seems interested in just hearing my experience, my doubts, my journey. The church seems threatened by good questions. It just makes me really fed up. I mean, is the church supposed to be a place for seekers, or is it only for finders? If it's for finders, I don't want anything to do with it.

Pastor: I hear your frustration with the people you meet in church, and I think our views of what sort of a place church should be are probably pretty similar. But I want to help you focus on what you said you wanted to explore with me. Tell me more about the questions that are most important to you right now.

Commentary: The pastor communicates quite clearly that she is hearing Rudy's feelings. But they agreed in the previous session that the focus would be his doubts and theological struggles, not his experience in the church. The two are, of course, related, but to maintain the agreed-upon focus, the pastor must be directive, not simply empathic.

The Strategic Pastoral Counseling Relationship Must Be a Partnership

To accomplish its goals in a brief period of time, strategic pastoral counseling must be built on a partnership of pastor and parishioner. Both parties must work together and in the same direction.

The partnership begins in the first moments of the first session as the pastor approaches the parishioner, not as an expert who will solve the parishioner's problems but rather as one who will come alongside and join him or her in working toward new understandings and fresh appropriations of resources for coping with troublesome life experiences. This working together involves agreement on the nature of the central problem that will be the primary focus of the counseling sessions, as well as agreement on the goals for change. Both parties are active participants in this process. Strategic pastoral counseling is the outworking of an alliance of pastor and parishioner—or, more correctly—of pastor, parishioner, and God.

In this partnership, each party has an important role. The role of the parishioner is to explore the problem from the various vantage points suggested by the pastor with as much openness and honesty as possible, and to be as open and accepting as possible of the feelings encountered in doing so. The role of the pastor is to listen, focus, and direct the process while attending to both the parishioner and the Holy Spirit. The role of the Spirit is to guide the process and both individuals in ways that move the parishioner toward a deeper engagement with God and a richer appropriation of the fullness of the life of the Spirit in the midst of present life circumstances.

Strategic Pastoral Counseling Must Concentrate on One Central and Specific Problem

The single most important difference between short- and long-term counseling is that short-term counseling deals primarily with only one problem. In this regard, brief, time-limited counseling is comparable to taking your car to a garage for an oil change, as opposed to leaving it with a mechanic with the instruction, "Check it out and fix anything that needs repair."

Strategic pastoral counseling focuses on only one aspect of life experience. It differs in this respect from the more ongoing relationship of spiritual direction in which the goal is the development of spiritual maturity. Strategic pastoral

51

counseling has a much more modest goal—examining a particular problem or life experience in the light of God's will for the person seeking help and attempting to facilitate movement toward growth and healing in and through present life circumstances. While this is still an ambitious goal, its focused nature makes it quite attainable within a short period of time.

Identifying the problem that will form the focus of counseling must be the primary concern of the individual seeking help. It is not the pastor's job to make this determination. Rather, this is part of the collaborative work that must be done by both pastor and parishioner. The pastor's job is, however, to ensure that the central concern is identified and that it is framed in a relatively specific manner.

For example, someone seeking counseling may in the first session talk about marital dissatisfaction, unresolved grief over the death of a friend, and vocational uncertainty. Which of these should be the central concern? The answer can be given only by the individual, and it can be given only after the matter is discussed with that person. The pastor may offer an opinion about what concern may be central and the best focus for the counseling sessions. Ultimately, however, this focus must be achieved by mutual consent.

The pastor's job in this regard is to push for clarification about this primary concern. Rudy—the man seeking help with what he called a "crisis of faith"—began the first session by offering excuses for his poor church attendance, talking about a book he had recently been reading, and grumbling about how judgmental his wife was about what she viewed as his increasingly liberal theological views. After listening for a few moments, the pastor continued:

Pastor: It sounds as though your feelings about the church or, maybe more particularly, your thoughts and beliefs about God may be the core of what you are hoping to talk with me about. Am I getting that right?

Rudy: Actually, it's much more my thoughts about God. I guess they are connected to my feelings about the church, but what I hope we can talk about are the things I don't seem to believe any longer. I don't want you to try to tell me what I should believe. What I'm hoping is that you can give me permission to doubt—that and the ability to share my doubts and beliefs with you would be a real gift. Does that sound reasonable?

It is also important that the focus be specific. "I'm dissatisfied with life" is too vague to be helpful, as is "I'm unhappy with my relationships." "I need help with my depression" or "I need help understanding why I feel dissatisfied in my marriage" is much more appropriate. One specific concern that makes sense to both pastor and parishioner must be identified, and, as will be discussed further in the next chapter, this concern should be identified no later than the end of the first session.

Time Limitation Must Be Maintained

One of the most difficult aspects of counseling for most pastors is setting necessary limits for the relationship. Limits are a God-ordained part of life, not a mere concession to life in the fast lane of the twenty-first century. In the long run, counseling is never helpful if limits are consistently ignored. Limit setting is, therefore, a part of all responsible counseling.

Temporal limits are not the only limits of strategic pastoral counseling. Wise counselors do not offer counseling to family members or to those with whom they do business. Nor do they offer counseling to people they are frightened of, uncomfortable with, or sexually attracted to. They are also aware that they are often not the ideal person to help those with whom they feel a strong identification. Strong negative reactions from the person consulting them are sometimes also a good reason for a referral to a colleague.

The primary limit in strategic pastoral counseling, however, is the temporal limit of five sessions. This number is based on the average number of sessions used by pastors when counseling parishioners. While it may feel ruthless to terminate one's counseling after five sessions, doing so will almost never pose serious problems for a parishioner and will ultimately be seen as a prudent rule that has significant advantages.

The limit of five sessions should be communicated no later than the first session and preferably when discussing a time for the first session. This should be done by means of a brief and direct statement such as the following: "I should let you know that my counseling is short-term and that I work within a maximum of five sessions. We will decide exactly how frequently we should meet once we first get together, but I want you to know my overall approach before we begin." A statement along these lines will almost always be well received. In fact, it will be a comfort to those who thought counseling involved a long-term commitment. The small percentage of people who are looking for a long-term relationship with their pastor will receive this news with disappointment, but it will put them on notice that they should come to the first counseling session ready to work or else not bother to come at all.

But what about the people who need more than five sessions of help? These people should be referred to someone who is appropriately qualified. Preparation for referral should then be a goal of the five sessions. (This will be discussed in the next chapter.) Long-term counseling is available from a number of groups of professional therapists, and a pastor should be aware of potential referral sources within the community.

Another implication of the five-session limit is that, as is the case with tune-ups for a car, a person seeking help may be back at some point in the future for further help. There is no assumption that strategic pastoral counseling fixes people for life. But setting a limit on the number of sessions discourages the formation of dependent relationships and encourages people to continue to work on their problems, returning for additional help in the future if that is what they need. To switch analogies, this pattern is akin to the way in which we relate to physicians. Typically, we go to our family doctor when we have symptoms that concern us, and we expect medical help for those specific problems. When we face additional problems, we go back again. This is also the method of strategic pastoral counseling. It is short-term and focused, and—with very few exceptions—it does not need to take more than five sessions. One important note about the limit is that these five sessions do not have to correspond to a period of five weeks. In fact, many pastors find weekly sessions to be less useful than sessions scheduled two or three weeks apart. Spacing out the last sessions is particularly helpful and should be considered even if the first sessions are held weekly. Less frequent sessions provide the parishioner with more of an opportunity to apply the things talked about in a session and then to use subsequent sessions to process these life experiences.

A secondary time limitation that must be enforced in strategic pastoral counseling is the length of sessions. Session lengths should be standardized and maintained. Failure to do so should be recognized not as flexibility and compassion but rather as an inability to provide the necessary structure for counseling. Seldom is it productive to go longer than ninety minutes, and most pastors find anything shorter than thirty minutes to be of minimal usefulness. Although the one-hour norm has, therefore, advantages that go beyond mere custom, there is nothing sacred about fifty- or sixty-minute sessions. What is important is establishing a standard session length that works and then maintaining this limit.

Holistic Counseling

It might seem surprising to suggest that a counseling approach that is short-term should also be holistic. But this is both possible and highly desirable.

The plurality of worldviews associated with the recent popularity of the term *holistic* have made some Christians forget that treating people as wholes—not a collection of parts—is a profoundly Christian thing to do. Biblical psychology is clearly a holistic psychology (Benner 1988, 1998). The various "parts" of persons (i.e., body, soul, spirit, heart, flesh, etc.) are not separate faculties or independent components of persons but different ways of seeing whole persons. Biblical discussions of persons emphasize first and foremost our essential unity of being. Humans are ultimately understandable only in the light of this primary and irreducible wholeness, and helping efforts that are truly Christian must resist the temptation to see persons only through their thoughts, feelings, behaviors, or any other manifestation of being. The alternative to holistic counseling involves focusing on only one of these modalities of functioning. Unfortunately, this is precisely what many approaches to counseling do—each tending to focus on one limited sphere of human functioning and ignoring the others. Thus, for example, behavior therapists focus on behavior, cognitive therapists on thinking, experiential therapists on feelings, and psychoanalytic therapists on the unconscious. Unfortunately, Christian approaches to counseling have often not fared much better. Adams's nouthetic counseling focuses on behavior (Adams 1970), and Crabb's biblical counseling focuses on thoughts (Crabb 1977).

In contrast, strategic pastoral counseling asserts that pastoral counseling must be fully and equally responsive to the behavioral (action), cognitive (thought), and affective (feeling) elements of personal functioning. Each examined separately can obscure what is really going on with a person. Taken together, however, they form the basis for a comprehensive assessment and effective intervention. Strategic pastoral counseling provides a framework for ensuring that each of these spheres of functioning is addressed, and this framework provides much of the structure for the counseling.

Structured Counseling

Long-term psychotherapy has often been compared to a game of chess in that, while we can describe in considerable detail the opening and closing moves, the great bulk of the process is much more difficult to describe. Thus, while the activities involved in both the initial assessment and the termination process can be specified reasonably clearly by long-term counselors, it is much more difficult to describe exactly what should be done in each of the intervening sessions. In contrast, short-term counseling is generally more structured. It is this structure that makes the brief nature of such counseling interventions possible. Each of the sessions has a clear focus, and each builds on the previous ones in contributing to the accomplishment of the overall goals.

The framework that structures strategic pastoral counseling is sufficiently tight so that a pastor can provide a holistic assessment and counseling intervention within a maximum of five sessions. But it is also sufficiently flexible to allow for differences in individual styles of counselors. This is important because counseling is not primarily a set of techniques but an intimate encounter and dialogue between two people. While this encounter is structured by rules that differ in many ways from those that structure other personal relationships, it is nonetheless highly personal. It necessarily involves the expression of a counselor's personality, and because of this, no two counselors should ever be expected to work in precisely the same way.

Good counseling always, therefore, involves a marriage of structure and freedom. Rules, techniques, and theory provide structure but also must allow for the expression of individuality. Good counselors are highly disciplined in how they structure their helping relationships. However, this discipline and structure become integrated within their personality and should not obscure the person behind the role. Nor should the structure be necessarily visible to the one receiving the counseling. It is, however, important. Counselors who eschew all structure tend to be undisciplined in their counseling. The overvaluation of freedom and flexibility results in unfocused counseling that tends to become long-term by default, not by plan.

The structure of strategic pastoral counseling grows out of the attempt to address the feelings, thoughts, and behaviors that are a part of the troubling experiences of the person seeking help. The structure is also responsive to the various tasks that face the counselor—tasks such as conducting an initial assessment, developing a general understanding of the problem and of the person's major needs, and selecting and delivering interventions and resources that will bring help. This structure is discussed in more detail in the next chapter.

Homework-Based Counseling

If strategic pastoral counseling is to achieve something of value within five sessions, the parishioner must come to each session ready to do productive work. Work done between sessions is an important way of maintaining momentum and providing real-life experiences that can be examined during the counseling sessions.

Homework can take a great variety of forms. Some strategic pastoral counselors emphasize reading that will aid understanding of the issues being explored. Bibliotherapy—or the therapeutic use of reading—has a long and honorable history in Christian soul care. Over two-thirds of the pastors contacted in the background research for the first edition of this book said they loan or give books to those they counsel, and informal feedback from those who have adopted the approach in the last decade suggests that at least the same percentage continue to do so.

The Bible itself is, of course, a rich bibliotherapeutic resource, and the encouragement of its reading throughout the history of the church clearly reflects the awareness that it can be a unique source of healing, sustenance, and guidance. The use of the Bible in such a manner is as ancient as the books of which it is composed. The wisdom literature of the Old Testament and the pastoral epistles of the New Testament were both originally written for spiritual guidance and nourishment. The Bible's use in counseling must be disciplined and selective, and particular care must be taken to ensure that it is never employed in a mechanical or impersonal manner. When used appropriately, however, the Bible can be one of the most dynamic and powerful resources available to the pastor who counsels.

But while the Bible is a unique therapeutic resource, it is not the only one. Many pastors report giving and loaning devotional and inspirational literature. In recent years, I have given or loaned so many copies of Henri Nouwen's *Return of the Prodigal Son* (1994) that I wish I had bought them in bulk. Larry Crabb's recent books (1997, 2001) have also been very well received, as have books by A. W. Tozer, Eugene Peterson, Brennan Manning, and Richard Rohr. These are just a few of my personal favorites. You will undoubtedly have your own list.

Books that deal with a particular problem or experience are also helpful. Among those I have personally used are Lewis Smedes's *Forgive and Forget* (1984), Philip Yancey's *Disappointment with God* (1988), C. S. Lewis's *Problem of Pain* (1940) and *A Grief Observed* (1961), and Diogenes Allen's *Traces of God in a Frequently Hostile World* (1981). Books originally prepared to accompany this volume[1] have also provided a significant extension of the face-to-face counseling of many strategic pastoral counselors.

However, reading is not the only work that can be assigned between sessions. Some strategic pastoral counselors use behavioral rehearsal—having a parishioner practice skills (i.e., assertiveness) or behaviors (i.e., making a speech or asking for a raise) that he or she wishes to implement in real life. Others encourage journaling as a way to aid prayerful reflection on experience. Having a counselee share things being explored and learned in the counseling process with carefully selected and trusted others is also often very helpful. Even something as simple as encouraging a parishioner to take time between sessions to review the previous session and come prepared to report what was beneficial or not beneficial helps maintain momentum and connect what happens in the pastor's office to what happens during the rest of the week.

Homework is not absolutely essential. Some pastors simply find it does not fit their personal style and are able to maintain sufficient focus and momentum without it. However,

---

1. See the additional reading section at the end of this and the next chapter for titles of some of these.

the majority of strategic pastoral counselors report that it is highly beneficial to have parishioners do things between sessions related to the work being undertaken, even if this involves nothing more than asking the parishioner what he or she feels would be most helpful to do before the next session.

Church-Based Counseling

It should be clear by now that strategic pastoral counseling involves more than a pastor running a private counseling practice out of a church office. The pastoral component of strategic pastoral counseling requires a much more integral and meaningful connection to the church. Once again there are a variety of ways in which this can be done. The bottom line, however, is that the counseling, not just the pastor, must be church-based.

Minimally, this means that the congregation understands and affirms the pastor's counseling as an important part of the total work of the church. Although it is obviously essential to preserve confidentiality, it may be helpful for the pastor to share something of the nature of his or her counseling with others in leadership so that they can support it in prayer and in other ways that may be appropriate.

Beyond this, the congregation should develop a variety of non-counseling supports for people who seek pastoral counseling. Support groups of various sorts are becoming a part of many congregations that seek to provide a dynamic ministry to their community. These can range from groups that focus on specific problems (e.g., alcohol or drugs, childhood sexual abuse, bereavement, or divorce) to those with a more general focus or for those going through normal life stages (e.g., grief and loss, parenting, marital communication and intimacy, job transitions, or retirement). Bible studies, fellowship groups, and other congregational care and ministry groups are all resources that can supplement strategic pastoral counseling.

One of the most important ways strategic pastoral counselors can maintain the short-term nature of their counseling is by connecting the person seeking help with others in the church who can provide portions of that help. For example, a pastor may connect a single mother with someone in the congregation who can provide assistance with basic tasks and responsibilities such as day care, financial planning, home repair, or transportation. Or a young couple may be connected with an older couple who, through friendship and modeling, may be able to help them with their marital struggles. To illustrate this, consider how a pastor connected Kevin—a young man in his early twenties—with people in the congregation.

Kevin first spoke to the pastor following a Sunday service and identified himself as new in the city and a visitor to the church. Rev. Fernando told him she was pleased he had come and encouraged him to call any time if there was anything she or the church could do to help him. Two days later Kevin did just that, telling Rev. Fernando that he wanted to get together to talk if she had time to see him.

In the session that followed a few days later, Kevin told Rev. Fernando that he had just started university, that this was his first time away from home, and that he was feeling really lonely. He also told her that he had trouble meeting friends and had always been somewhat of a loner. Church had always been a place where he felt accepted and that was why he had made an effort to start looking for a home congregation as soon as he had moved. He then spent much of the remainder of the hour talking about his family, the first week at school, and his plans for the future.

Partway through this session, Rev. Fernando began to assume that this was probably going to be a single-session counseling encounter. When she asked Kevin what he had been hoping for when he called her, he said he had just wanted to talk and maybe get a better sense of whether this church might work for him as a home church. He seemed to have no problem that he wished to discuss in a more extended fashion and told her that he had not expected more than one meeting.

Rev. Fernando saw this contact as an opportunity to do something much more valuable than merely recruit a new member for the congregation. As Kevin's story began to unfold, her thinking turned to people in the congregation with whom she could put Kevin in contact. Although he could possibly benefit from counseling—perhaps focusing on the long-standing difficulty he had forming friendships—what he wanted at the moment was a friend, not counseling. Her offer at the end of the session was, therefore, to introduce Kevin to several other students at his university from within the congregation. She said she would be glad to do so either next Sunday, if he wished to attend, or at any other time or location.

Even if Kevin had decided to pursue counseling regarding the difficulty he has making friends, he might still have benefited from being connected with potential friends. Others benefit from—and welcome—an offer of introduction to someone within the congregation who, like them, has recently lost a child, been diagnosed with cancer, experienced a divorce, or had problems with their children. The most appropriate contact for others might be someone who may be able to help with a job, who might share an interest, who seems to be on a similar spiritual journey, or who shares an ethnic or national identity.

Spiritually Focused Counseling

The sixth distinctive of strategic pastoral counseling is that it is spiritually focused. All counseling has some sort of focus, the focus being whatever has the highest priority. Various models of contemporary counseling emphasize such things as relationships or relational patterns, early childhood experiences, repressed feelings, bodily awareness, or automatic thoughts. Any of these serves to guide a counselor in knowing what to emphasize and what to ignore. Without such guidelines, counseling drifts aimlessly and accomplishes little. The focus provides the central organizing purpose and direction.

To describe the focus of strategic pastoral counseling as spiritual is to note that the focus is on the person in relation to God. This requires that the pastoral counselor be attentive to the way in which God is already active in the person's life and the way in which the person is responding to this activity. But before we examine this more fully, let me first say something about the concept of spirituality.

Contemporary use of the term *spirituality* is highly varied. Some of the ambiguity surrounding the concept is semantic and can be avoided by careful use of language. However, much of the ambiguity is unavoidable. Spirituality brings us up against some of the most complex mysteries of our being. In the words of May, "Spirit and mystery are closely related. . . . Mystery may not always be spiritual but there is no doubt that spirituality is always mysterious" (May 1982, 32). Even with the most precisely formulated definition of the concept, we will, therefore, face inevitable ambiguity in making the spiritual aspect of persons the focus of strategic pastoral counseling.

The concept of spirituality is grounded in the existence of God as Spirit and his loving act of having created us in his image for intimate relationship with him. The human spirit is not a part of us, separate from other nonspiritual parts. Rather, it is that which defines our humanness and is foundational to our being. In the words of St. Augustine's famous prayer, "Thou hast made us for thyself, and our hearts are restless until they find their rest in thee." Although this restlessness is not always experienced as a spiritual longing, it is present at the deepest levels of our being and gives direction to the totality of our personality. To be a human person is to be a spiritual being. We differ from one another not in whether or not we are spiritual but in the nature of our spirituality.

Our spiritual nature is a deep and foundational part of who we are as humans. It is a matter of the heart. As used in biblical anthropology, the heart lies at the center of our personality and is the point of integration for our being. The essential commitments and directions of life are expressed in the orientation of the heart, and spirituality refers to the heart orientation that underlies and directs the rest of our being. Humans are incurably spiritual. Created for surrender to and loving service of God, we are given only the choice of whom to surrender to and serve. The basic spiritual direction of personality—that is, surrender to and service of God or rebellion against him and service of a lesser god—is reflected in all aspects of our functioning.

What, then, is involved in making spiritual matters the primary focus of counseling? First and foremost it means that the strategic pastoral counselor must recognize that before he or she enters the life of the individual seeking pastoral assistance, God is already present and active in that life. This is a core assumption of spiritual direction and is one of the most important things pastoral counselors can learn from this closely related soul-care tradition. If a pastoral counselor assumes God's presence and activity, he or she will look for clues of both. In so doing, the counselor helps the one seeking help develop an attitude of prayer—for what is prayer if it is not attentiveness to God.

Counselors will find whatever they are looking for. If they are looking for psychopathology, they will find it. If they are looking for unconscious problems, they will find them. And if they are looking for the presence and activity of God in a person's life, they will—with the assistance of God's Spirit—find them.

But while God is active in seeking to draw all men and women closer to himself, much of the time most of us are unaware of his gracious presence and acts of love. Nor are people always even aware of their deep spiritual longings. Making spiritual matters the primary focus of counseling is aided by recognizing that people do not have to be talking about God to be expressing something about their spirituality. Struggles associated with the search for meaning in life or with the quest for identity, wholeness, or even fulfillment all contain spiritual elements. But so do problems that seem on the surface to be more mundane, problems such as depression, marital conflicts, or anxiety. Once pastoral counselors begin to understand the diverse ways in which people mask their experience of and response to the spiritual quest, they can become more discerning of the presence of the spiritual in the problems presented in counseling.

Learning to discern the presence of the spiritual begins by understanding that spirituality manifests itself in the broad context of life experiences, not merely in religious experiences. Therefore, regardless of the problem a parishioner has, it has spiritual implications. The problem must be taken seriously, for it is the context in which spiritual issues can be most readily discerned and in which spiritual resources are most needed.

While spiritual issues are often masked by other seemingly nonspiritual concerns, they are also often presented more directly—oftentimes by means of theological questions. A strategic pastoral counselor should listen for the underlying personal meaning of such questions. Thus, when one requests help in understanding a doctrine such as providence, the counselor should quickly move from a discussion of theology to an exploration of the reasons for the question. The way in which theological issues are most appropriately addressed in pastoral counseling is by moving from theological generalities to spiritual particularities. What specific personal experiences led the parishioner to ask about the nature of God's intentions toward him or her? While accepting the validity of the question about providence, the pastor should also be alert to the deeper and more personal experiences and questions that lurk behind the question.

Learning to focus on the spiritual means learning to listen to the story behind the story. This deeper narrative is often missed, not because parishioners seek to hide what most needs to be communicated but because more often they themselves do not know the nature of their deepest concerns and feelings. In fact, for some people, the major benefit of successful counseling is that the one seeking counseling comes to know more clearly his or her own story. The story behind the story is a story of ultimate concerns, basic anxieties, foundational commitments, and fundamental beliefs. It is a story of the heart.

But listening to the story behind the story requires that a pastor first listen to and take seriously the story as it is told.

65

This story cannot be disregarded as the pastor listens to discern the underlying spiritual issues. Doing so would be a failure to take the parishioner's problem seriously and would make a mockery of counseling as genuine dialogue.

The strategic pastoral counselor listens to and enters into the experience of the parishioner as the parishioner relates his or her struggles with illness, betrayal, confusion, loss, financial reversal, or vocational uncertainty. But while this is a real part of the story, it is not the whole story that must be heard and understood, for in the midst of this story emerges another, the story of the person's spiritual response to the experience. This response may be one of unwavering trust in God but a failure to expect much of him. Or it may be one of doubt, anger, confusion, or despair. Or God may be seen as largely irrelevant to the present circumstances. He may be a forgotten part of personal life experience. Each of these is a spiritual response to present struggles. In one form or another, the spiritual aspect of the person's experience will always be discernible to the pastor who watches for it.

I have elsewhere described the human spiritual quest as the deep-seated longing for place, a quest to find where we belong (Benner 1998). The task of the pastoral counselor can be seen as helping others understand the places they have selected as their spiritual homes as well as the implications of their choices. Most Christians are unaware of both their deep longing for a place and the compromise places they have accepted. They may think they have made Christ their spiritual home, but in reality they have also accepted other places of soul rest. Perhaps their worth comes from their accomplishments, not simply from being deeply loved by God. Or perhaps their security comes more from their financial assets than from their rest in the Lord. They know only their dis-ease, and they seek relief from it. It is the strategic pastoral counselor's job to help them understand the meaning of this dis-ease, not merely to give the relief they seek. This is what is involved in listening for the spiritual.

In summary, focusing on spiritual matters does not mean merely watching for opportunities to shift the conversation to religious topics. Spirituality has to do with our ultimate allegiances and investments. Sometimes these will correspond closely to expressed religious beliefs, values, and commitments. At other points, however, there may be quite a gap between religious behaviors and spiritual realities. The focus of strategic pastoral counseling should be on the latter.

Explicitly Christian Counseling

While it is important not to confuse spirituality with religiosity, it is equally important not to confuse Christian spirituality with any of its imitations. In this regard, it is crucial that strategic pastoral counseling be distinctively and explicitly Christian.

Not all spirituality is Christian spirituality, and although strategic pastoral counseling begins with a focus on spiritual matters broadly understood, its primary goal is to facilitate a person's awareness of and response to the call of God to surrender and service. This is the essential and most important aspect of strategic pastoral counseling.

Anyone seeking help from a pastoral counselor should be aware that the pastoral counselor stands committed to the belief that ultimate wholeness cannot be found apart from a restored relationship with God through Jesus Christ. Pastoral counseling is the facilitation of this wholeness through dialogue and interaction that are designed to nurture life in and through the Spirit.

One of the ways in which strategic pastoral counseling is made explicitly Christian is through its use of religious resources such as prayer, Scripture, and the sacraments. As pointed out earlier, these resources must never be used in a mechanical, legalistic, or magical fashion. Employed sensitively and wisely, however, they can be the means of bringing a parishioner more closely in touch with the God who is the source of all life, growth, and healing. Nothing less than this should ever be the reason for using religious resources.

While theological language can be a distraction and used to avoid genuine dialogue, it can also be a potentially important resource in strategic pastoral counseling. Counseling should never be reduced to doctrinal instruction. However, both theological reflection and discourse are appropriate, and discussing theological concepts can be a helpful way of facilitating such discourse and reflection.

A concept such as sin can be used as either a power ploy and guilt manipulation strategy (i.e., "What you are telling me is that you are living in sin.") or as a way of introducing a divine perspective on the topic under discussion (i.e., "The brokenness you are describing forms a central part of what Scripture means by sin. It is precisely here that God wants to meet you and heal you."). Similarly, providence, sovereignty, the incarnation, and a great variety of other theological concepts all point to Christian understandings of life that have valuable pastoral and spiritual implications. These pastoral and spiritual implications form the most legitimate reason for using theological language and discourse in strategic pastoral counseling.

A final and possibly even more fundamental way in which strategic pastoral counseling is Christian is that it encourages reliance on the Holy Spirit. The Spirit is the indispensable source of all wisdom, which is necessary for the practice of pastoral counseling. As obvious as this may seem, it has generally not been emphasized or even discussed in pastoral counseling literature. In one notable exception, Oates reminds us that since the Holy Spirit is the true Counselor (John 14:26), he should be seen as the pastoral counselor's assistant (Oates 1962). Recognizing that all healing and growth are ultimately of God, a pastor can relax in the work of pastoral counseling. The ultimate responsibility for the person lies with God.

Oates notes that this counseling role of the Holy Spirit begins with a personal ministry to the pastor and extends through the pastor into the counseling relationship with the parishioner. As the pastor learns to rely on the Spirit for daily strength, direction, and wisdom, he or she develops a sort of dependence that is appropriate in a pastoral counseling relationship. The pastor can rely on the Spirit of God to help both parties in the counseling relationship know what to say and when to say it. Oates suggests that Jesus' words to his disciples in Matthew 10:19–20 ("Do not worry about how to speak or what to say; what you are to say will be given to you when the time comes; because it is not you who will be speaking; the Spirit of your Father will be speaking in you."), while originally referring to the persecution that they were to experience, are equally applicable to pastors facing a counseling session (1962, 62–63). Oates calls this the ministry of the Holy Spirit to the pastor facing the anxiety of communication. But this same help is also available to the parishioner. The pastor can encourage those seeking help to pray before sessions for guidance about what should be discussed and for recall of important matters that should be shared. This is particularly helpful advice for the somewhat obsessive individual who comes with a list of concerns to discuss, anxious lest something be left unsaid. Both the parishioner and the pastor should learn to trust that the Spirit of God will guide the communication process.

A related role of the Holy Spirit in pastoral counseling is indicated in the promise that the Spirit will bring to mind all that Jesus has taught (John 14:26). This teaching ministry of the Spirit is indispensable for pastoral counseling, and the pastor should remember that it is the Spirit, not he or she, who has this primary role. The same is true with regard to the promise that it is the Spirit who convicts of sin (John 16:8). This is a crucial matter in pastoral counseling, one that is surrounded by much confusion. The question is often put in terms of whether the pastor should take a nonjudgmental attitude toward sinful behavior or a posture of condemning sin and thereby upholding the standard of God's law. But this question confuses the issue. Everything we know about the dynamics of therapeutic conversation indicates that a nonjudgmental attitude of accepting love is foundational to effective counseling. But this does not mean that the conviction of sin does not or should not take place. Rather, it means that the conviction of sin is the work of the Spirit of God. Genuine conviction is always the inner accomplishment of God's Spirit. The best a pastor can accomplish by condemning sin is neurotic feelings of guilt, which are a poor substitute for genuine conviction of sin.

Strategic pastoral counselors do not content themselves, therefore, by focusing on generic spirituality. Their goal is the enhancement of distinctively Christian spirituality and the accompanying wholeness of being that is possible in and through life in the Spirit. We turn now to the way in which this is accomplished in the three stages of strategic pastoral counseling.

Additional Readings

Benner, D. 1998. *Care of souls: Revisioning Christian nurture and counsel.* Grand Rapids: Baker. This book contains a more extensive discussion of the relationship between spiritual and psychological dynamics of functioning, as well as the way in which pastors can learn to discern the presence of the spiritual in the midst of whatever aspects of living are being discussed.

Childs, B. 1990. *Short-term pastoral counseling.* Nashville: Abingdon. Presents an interesting overview of a short-term model of pastoral counseling that employs ten sessions and focuses on what is described as the "focal relational problem" of the parishioner.

Green, D., and M. Lawrenz. 1996. *Encountering shame and guilt.* Grand Rapids: Baker. An application of strategic pastoral counseling to problems of shame and guilt that includes several detailed case studies.

Kollar, C. 1997. *Solution-focused pastoral counseling.* Grand Rapids: Zondervan. A brief approach to pastoral counseling that, as its name suggests, focuses on solutions rather than problems. It draws its inspiration from the more general solution-focused counseling approach that has recently gained considerable attention, an approach that builds on helping people identify the resources they already possess to effect changes.

Oates, W. 1962. *Protestant pastoral counseling.* Philadelphia: Westminster. This book contains much that is helpful, particularly a good discussion of the role of the Holy Spirit in pastoral counseling.

Rassieur, C. L. 1988. *Pastor, our marriage is in trouble: A guide to short-term counseling.* Philadelphia: Westminster. A highly structured five-session approach to short-term pastoral marital counseling that shares many of the emphases of strategic pastoral counseling but that, thus far, is applied only to work with marital problems.

Sharp, J. 1999. Solution-focused counseling: A model for parish ministry. *Journal of Pastoral Care* 53, no. 1:71–79. Presents another account of a solution-focused approach to pastoral counseling.

Welch, E., and G. Shogren. 1995. *Addictive behavior.* Grand Rapids: Baker. Another application of strategic pastoral counseling, this time to addictions frequently encountered by pastors.

Westberg, G. 1979. *Theological roots of wholistic health care.* Hinsdale, Ill.: Wholistic Health Centers. Although this book uses the older, variant spelling of holistic, the argument the author makes for the theological foundation of a wholistic approach to persons applies equally well to strategic pastoral counseling and other approaches employing the newer spelling.

Worthington, E., and K. Worthington. 1996. *Helping parents make disciples.* Grand Rapids: Baker. This application of strategic pastoral counseling focuses on parenting problems. The book includes a number of case studies and other helpful, practical information on how to work with parents seeking pastoral help with their children.

4

The Stages and Tasks
of Strategic Pastoral Counseling

The three stages of strategic pastoral counseling can be described as *encounter, engagement,* and *disengagement.* While many counseling models describe their stages by such task-oriented terms as problem definition, goal development, and intervention, relational language better reflects the essentially personal nature of counseling. Counseling is not something one person does *to* another person. Rather, it is something one does *with* another person. The essence of Christian soul care is lost when we view counseling as something mechanical or technical. It is, in essence, something deeply personal and relational. It is a relationship built around dialogue and genuine encounter.

The first stage of strategic pastoral counseling, *encounter,* corresponds to the initial meeting of a pastor and the one seeking help. At this point, the pastor's goal is to establish a personal contact with the person, set the boundaries for the counseling relationship, become acquainted with the person and his or her central concerns, conduct a pastoral diagnosis, and develop a mutually acceptable focus for the work they will do together. In the second stage, *engagement,* the pastor and the parishioner roll up their sleeves and get down to the hard work of counseling. This normally occupies the next one to three sessions[1] and involves the exploration of the person's feelings, thoughts, and behavioral patterns associated with the problem area, as well as the development of new perspectives and strategies for coping or change. The third and final stage, *disengagement,* occurs in the last one or possibly two sessions and involves an evaluation of progress and an assessment of remaining concerns, a referral for further help if this is needed, and the termination of the counseling relationship. These stages and tasks are summarized in table 5.

Table 5

The Stages and Tasks of Strategic Pastoral Counseling

The Encounter Stage
Joining and boundary setting
Exploring the central concerns and relevant history
Conducting a pastoral diagnosis
Achieving a mutually agreeable focus for counseling

The Engagement Stage
Exploring the affective, cognitive, and behavioral aspects of the
  problem and identifying the resources for coping or change

The Disengagement Stage
Evaluating progress and assessing remaining concerns
Arranging a referral (if needed)
Terminating counseling

---

1. In this coordination of tasks and stages with counseling sessions, I am assuming a course of counseling that involves five sessions. In reality, however, strategic pastoral counseling often involves fewer sessions and is frequently concluded in as few as one or two sessions. Although all tasks are still addressed in such very brief counseling encounters, the stages run together fluidly.

The Encounter Stage

Encounter is a term sometimes used to refer to an unexpected or casual contact—for example, a chance encounter between two strangers on a train. This meaning, however, misses the richness of the concept. As used by Buber (1965), an encounter refers to a meeting of two people who relate to each other not as an impersonal "it" but as a personal "thou." It is this deeply personal meaning that describes the first stage of strategic pastoral counseling.

The foundation of a helpful pastoral encounter lies in the personal qualities of the pastor. Three characteristics are especially important: empathy, respect, and authenticity.[2] Although these are valuable traits in and of themselves, in strategic pastoral counseling, they are not the end but the means to the end. The end is a relationship in which two people meet in a place of respect and dialogue and by so doing increase their attentiveness and responsiveness to the Spirit of God, who is the third party in the encounter.

Empathy, respect, and authenticity, while ways of relating helpfully to others, are not mere techniques. Empathy is not something one does. It is not merely a formula for listening. Rather, empathy is a posture of openness to the experience of another person and may be communicated by reflecting back to the other person what one is hearing. Respect involves communicating a deep valuing of the other. Ideally, it involves the absence of judgmentalism and conditional acceptance. Respect is not a denial of personal judgments, for these are an inevitable and important part of human functioning. It is, however, a result of seeing a fellow human as God does—as an image bearer of God and therefore a person of extreme worth, even if this image is marred by brokenness and distorted by sin. Finally, authenticity is a state of being real or genuine. It is the foundation for both empathy and respect. Together these three

2. This foundation is well described by Rogers (1961), and a thoughtful theological perspective on these therapeutic qualities is presented by Oden (1966).

qualities form the bedrock of any pastoral encounter that is to become a genuinely helpful counseling relationship.

As noted earlier, the initial encounter of a pastoral counselor and a parishioner usually occurs prior to the first counseling session as a part of some other facet of pastoral care and ministry. The counseling encounter, though it differs in purpose and structure from the previous contact, builds on what has gone before.

Joining and Boundary Setting

The first tasks in this initial stage of strategic pastoral counseling are joining and boundary setting. Joining involves putting a parishioner at ease by means of a few moments of casual conversation. One way a pastor can do this is by noting similarities between his or her experience and that of the parishioner. Perhaps there is a similarity in age, ethnic or geographic background, aspects of education, or interests. If the pastor does not know the parishioner, a question or two about where he or she lives or works or about anything else (other than the reason for coming for counseling) is an excellent way to make this initial contact.

Consider the following as an example of joining through casual conversation:

Pastor: Good morning, Mr. Smith. I am Pastor Brown. I'm glad to meet you. Won't you step into my office? I have seen you in church, but I don't believe we've talked other than when you called to set up this appointment. Are you from this part of the city?

Mr. Smith: Actually, we live just around the corner from the church, but I wouldn't expect you to know me, as we just moved from New York three weeks ago.

Pastor: Really? I'm from this area originally, but my wife is from just outside New York. This must be a big adjustment for you.

Preliminary conversation of this sort should never take more than five minutes and can usually be kept to two or three. It is not always necessary. Some people are immediately ready to tell their story, and in such cases, there is no need for small talk. They have already joined with the pastor.

Boundary setting involves communicating the purpose of the first session and, if the pastor has not already done so, the time frame for the session and subsequent sessions. This can be handled with a simple explanation such as the following:

Pastor: I've set aside the next hour for you, and we can use as much of it as you want. My hope is that by the end of this time I will have some understanding of what brought you to see me and that both of us will have a sense as to whether we want to meet again. If we do choose to meet again, you should be aware that I conduct my counseling within a maximum of five sessions. But we can leave that until later. Perhaps you can begin by telling me what brings you to speak with me at this time.

If temporal boundaries (including the length of the sessions) were set before the first meeting, the pastor can begin with the last sentence of the above. The phrase "at this time" is important because it directs the parishioner toward what is called the presenting problem and encourages specificity. At this point, the pastor is not interested in the history of the person's concerns, only in their most immediate and present manifestation. The pastor wants to know what this person is hoping for or needs and why he or she sought counseling.

Exploring the Central Concerns and Relevant History

Inviting the parishioner to explain what brought him or her in at the present time is an important transition point and leads into the person's story. It also demonstrates that the pastor is responsible for these transitions. Pastoral counselors sometimes worry that transitions have to be smooth, so smooth that the parishioner is unaware that anyone is

77

providing direction. This is a serious misunderstanding of the nature of counseling. Transitions are necessary, are expected by the parishioner, are the responsibility of the pastor, and do not have to be introduced with the smoothness of a talk show host. All that is necessary is to say, "Now, tell me about such and such."

Either during the session or immediately after it has concluded, the pastor should write down the parishioner's explanation of what brought him or her to the pastor at the present time. As much as possible, it should be written down in the parishioner's exact words. For a variety of reasons, this preliminary statement of concerns is often one of the most difficult things the pastor will have to remember, but it is also one of the most important. The pastor should not lose sight of the way in which the parishioner understands the problem and what help he or she expects. This is not to say that these matters will not change over time. However, if they do, the pastor should be aware of such a change. The much less desirable alternative is that, having forgotten the initial concerns, the pastor simply drifts toward his or her own agenda of what the parishioner needs.

As the parishioner tells his or her story, the pastor's job is to listen carefully and empathically. Good listening also involves an effort to understand the parishioner's inner experience, communicated both verbally and nonverbally. Gentle probing and repeating what is heard are secondary but also important communication skills. They build on the foundation of empathic listening and encourage the parishioner to continue self-exploration and expression.

After hearing a statement of present concerns, the pastor will usually find it helpful to get a brief historical perspective on both these concerns and the person. Ten to fifteen minutes may be spent exploring the development of the concerns and the person's efforts to cope or get help with them. It is also important at this point to find out about the person's present living and family arrangements as well as his or her work or educational situation. Asking about such matters lets the parishioner know that the pastor is interested in him or her as a person, not just as a container of problems. Most people are quite glad to share this kind of information.

This exploration of the broader contextual aspects of the person must remain focused and directed. To keep it within ten to fifteen minutes, the pastor may have to cut off certain lines of conversation and leave some areas unexplored. Some matters can be noted as topics for future investigation, and the pastor may want to share this with the parishioner. But many others must simply be ignored. Giving direction to a conversation means focusing on certain things and ignoring others. This is a crucial skill that strategic pastoral counselors must learn.

The organizing thread for this historical and contextual section of the first session should be the presenting problem. If, for example, the presenting problem involves marital conflict, a history of the present and any previous marriages should be the focus. If the presenting problem involves grief associated with a recent loss, the history of the attachment and the loss should be explored.

Listening with a view to understanding and knowing the person is the goal of the first session. In this regard, the first session should not focus too narrowly on the presenting problem, lest the pastor end the session knowing a great deal about the problem but little about the person who is experiencing the problem. There must be a balance in focus between problem and person. It is easy to focus on concerns, but it is also necessary to know something of the person's strengths if counseling is to be helpful. A second balance must be maintained between the present and the past. A balanced focus on both is necessary if the pastor is to know enough about the past to understand adequately the person in the present.

Conducting a Pastoral Diagnosis

The concept of diagnosis is primarily associated with medicine. However, its literal meaning and historical usage make clear that the diagnostic task is an appropriate and essential part of pastoral counseling as well.

In an excellent book titled *The Minister as Diagnostician,* Pruyser argues that the first task of anyone who seeks to help another with a problem is some sort of problem definition (Pruyser 1976). The identification and labeling of a problem is an exercise in diagnosis, and pastors must do this just as surely as physicians. Pruyser defines diagnosis as "grasping things as they really are, so as to do the right thing" (30). Diagnosis is, therefore, an act of discernment, and a diagnostic judgment will always be present—either implicitly or explicitly—by the end of the first stage of counseling. Responsible pastoral counseling involves making a good diagnostic judgment about the nature of the problem. An implicit diagnostic judgment will guide counseling just as surely as an explicit one. The advantage of the latter, however, is that it is available for scrutiny and continuous reevaluation.

But by what criteria or conceptual scheme should pastoral diagnosis proceed? Many pastoral counselors, assuming that pastoral counseling bears a close enough similarity to psychological counseling, see the standard classification of psychiatric and psychological disorders as suitable for them as well. Thus, even if they do not conduct a comprehensive psychological or psychiatric evaluation, they take standard clinical understandings as their conceptual reference points for problem definition. They may feel, for example, that they have conducted a pastoral assessment and are ready to proceed with pastoral counseling after they have identified a person as displaying a narcissistic orientation, having a problem with repressed anger, or experiencing unconscious conflict over dependency longings. I would suggest, however, that while these sorts of psychological concepts can be helpful when making a pastoral assessment, they do not in themselves provide a meaningful pastoral diagnosis.

The pastoral diagnosis must be related primarily to the spiritual focus of pastoral counseling. Thus, the diagnosis that is called for in the first stage of counseling involves an assessment of a person's spiritual well-being. While this is intimately connected to a person's psychological well-being, the exclusive use of psychological categories and concepts makes it difficult to describe adequately a person's spiritual health or pathology. What we need, therefore, are categories for describing a person's spiritual functioning.

A first tentative step in the development of categories for the assessment of spiritual functioning by pastoral counselors was provided by Pruyser (1976). He suggested that seven broad dimensions of experience are relevant to understanding a person's spiritual functioning: an awareness of the holy, a sense of divine providence, the nature of faith, the sense of divine grace, the sense of remorse for sins, the sense of communion with others, and the sense of vocation.

While many pastors have found this framework for pastoral diagnosis to be helpful, Malony (1985, 1988) pointed out that its usefulness would be enhanced if it were made more distinctively Christian. He suggested beginning with a definition of Christian religious maturity and allowing the framework for assessing spiritual well-being to emerge from this. His starting point, therefore, was the following definition of Christian religious maturity:

> Mature Christians are those who have identity, integrity, and inspiration. They have "identity" in that their self-understanding is that they are children of God—created by God and destined to live according to a divine plan. They have "integrity" in that their daily life is lived in the awareness that they have been redeemed by God's grace from the guilt of sin and that they can freely respond to God's will in the present. They have "inspiration" in that they live with the sense that God is available to sustain, comfort, encourage, and direct their lives on a daily basis. These dimensions of maturity relate to belief in God the Father, God the Son, and God the Holy Spirit. They pertain to the Christian doctrines of creation, redemption, and sanctification. They provide the foundation for practical daily living. (Malony 1985, 28)

Based on this understanding of optimal Christian functioning and building on the work of Pruyser, Malony suggested eight areas of personal functioning that require assessment when evaluating Christian religious well-being. These eight dimensions are summarized in table 6 and form the basis of his structured "religious status interview."

Table 6

Dimensions of Pastoral Diagnosis

Awareness of God
Acceptance of God's grace
Repentance and responsibility
Response to God's leadership
Involvement in the church
Experience of fellowship
Ethics
Openness in faith
Adapted from Malony (1988)

By awareness of God, Malony means a person's attitude toward God. This includes the degree of awe or sense of "creatureliness" one feels in relation to God, the degree of dependence on God, the nature and quality of a person's relationship with Jesus, a person's experience of worship, and his or her practices and experiences of prayer.

The second dimension—acceptance of God's grace—involves the degree to which a person understands and experiences God's benevolence and unconditional love. This includes how the person experiences God's response to sin and how he or she understands God's role in personal suffering, experiences his love, and responds to his forgiveness.

The third dimension of a pastoral diagnosis is related to repentance and responsibility. This involves a person's understanding regarding what causes problems in life, motivation for repentance, experience with asking for and granting forgiveness, and the degree of responsibility taken for personal feelings and behaviors.

The fourth dimension involves the degree to which a person trusts in, hopes for, and lives out God's direction for his or her life. This includes how the person makes major decisions and thinks of the future and how faith is related to his or her various roles in the family, workplace, and community.

The fifth dimension focuses on a person's involvement in the church. According to Malony, this involves both the quantitative and qualitative nature of such involvement as well as the motivation for it. This dimension also includes a person's financial involvement.

The sixth dimension—the experience of fellowship—involves the degree to which a person experiences intimacy with other Christians, identification of self as a child of God, and identification with all humanity. The nature of a person's relationships within and outside the church is the major focus of exploration related to this dimension.

The seventh dimension—ethics—focuses not simply on what a person believes but also on how those beliefs translate into action. It includes ethical decision making, the ways in which personal faith influences a sense of right and wrong, and current ethical issues that are of personal concern.

The final dimension is openness in faith. By this Malony means the degree to which a person is growing spiritually and is open to the faith journey. This category includes matters related to openness to divergent viewpoints, the ways in which faith affects the various aspects of life, and commitment to the growth and development of personal faith.

When conducted in the structured form of the religious status interview, this approach to pastoral diagnosis consists of thirty-three open-ended questions and requires approximately one hour. Because most applications of strategic pastoral counseling do not allow for this amount of time for diagnosis, the formal use of the religious status interview is not recommended. However, the framework can be adapted by those desiring to conduct a brief, informal pastoral evaluation, and many pastors have reported its usefulness in this form.

Malony's dimensions of pastoral diagnosis should not be seen as a checklist for the first session. First and foremost they are a framework for listening and reflection; only secondarily are they a set of questions to be asked. One way to conduct this assessment of spiritual functioning is by means of a religious history. Physicians routinely take medical histories, and psychologists take psychological histories. It is only appropriate for clergy to inquire about a person's religious upbringing and pilgrimage. Exploration of this general area of religious functioning can then be guided either by Malony's categories or by other helpful ways of assessing personal spiritual well-being.

Because of the primacy of the assessment and facilitation of spiritual functioning in strategic pastoral counseling, an evaluation of spiritual well-being must be based on an ability to discern between healthy and unhealthy religiosity.[3] The following questions, adapted from those suggested by Clinebell (1984), can assist a pastor in assessing the overall health of a person's religious beliefs and practices:

1. Do they provide the person with a meaningful and robust philosophy of life?
2. Do they provide a set of values that serve as ethical guidelines for behavior?
3. Do they provide an experience of self-transcendence?
4. Do they inspire a love of life?
5. Do they provide for a renewal of the person's sense of basic trust?
6. Do they offer the person a positive experience of community?
7. Do they enhance self-acceptance and a positive sense of self-esteem?
8. Do they enhance the capacity for self-denial and altruistic self-sacrifice?
9. Do they encourage the vital energies of sex and assertiveness to be used in affirming, responsible ways rather than in repressive or destructive ways?
10. Do they foster hope?
11. Do they encourage acceptance of reality?
12. Do they provide a means of moving from guilt to reconciliation and forgiveness?

3. The unfortunate truth is that for some people religion does not serve as a force of growth, liberation, and healing. Rather, their faith and religious practices get mixed up with their pathology and actually operate as destructive dynamics in personality. Psychologists are familiar with this dynamic, and the reason that so much of what they say about religion is negative is that many of the people they see have pathological forms of religion. The classic discussion of these differing forms of religion is found in James (1902). More recent discussions can be found in Oates (1970) and Hill (1999).

13. Do they encourage the creative development and personalization of beliefs and values?
14. Do they enhance sensitivity to injustice and motivate the person to work toward justice?
15. Do they provide a way to face the inevitable losses of life, including the person's own death?
16. Do they foster an awareness of and appreciation for the mysteries of life?
17. Do they encourage a heightened aliveness, joy, and zest for living?
18. Do they provide for a renewal of the person's sense of belongingness in the universe?
19. Do they encourage a trusting surrender to God and a life of faith in and dependence on him?
20. Do they serve to integrate all aspects of personality, bringing the totality of personal functioning under the direction of fundamental religious commitments?

While this list is not a comprehensive framework for evaluating the health of a person's spiritual functioning, it does suggest some of the parameters of such an evaluation. It should also be made clear that, once again, these are not necessarily questions that need to be asked but questions that should guide a pastor as he or she listens. The pastor who listens to a person's story in light of these questions will inevitably develop a sense of how well the person's faith is serving him or her. With this assessment the pastor will be able to identify ways that subsequent sessions can be used to enhance the health-inducing qualities of faith and life in Christ.

Achieving a Mutually Agreeable Focus for Counseling

As mentioned earlier, strategic pastoral counseling requires that a pastor and parishioner be in agreement as to the basic problem or concern that will serve as the primary focus of their work together. Often this is self-evident, made immediately clear by the parishioner. For example, "Pastor, my wife just walked out on me for another man, and I am devastated!"

leaves little doubt about what the primary focus will be. On the other hand, some parishioners may report a wide range of concerns and questions in the first session. The pastor and parishioner must then identify and agree on the primary focus.

After doing so, they need to decide on the goals for counseling. These will at times be quite specific (e.g., to be able to make an informed decision about a potential job change) but at other times will be rather broad (e.g., to be able to cope with an illness). As these examples show, some goals will describe an end point, while others will describe a process. Maintaining flexibility in how goals are understood is crucial if strategic pastoral counseling is to be helpful for the broad range of situations encountered by pastors. It is also important if the approach is to accommodate their various counseling styles.

To summarize, strategic pastoral counseling requires a specific focus, but it does not make the same demand of goals. In other words, the pastor and the parishioner need to agree on what they will work on without necessarily committing to a specific outcome. This contrasts with some brief counseling approaches that require measurable behavioral goals (Thomas 1999).

The following conversation illustrates the process of identifying a focus and goals with someone who has a difficult time being specific about what she wants. In the first half of the first session, Diane touched on a broad range of things that were concerning her, including her relationship with her parents, a recent sense that God no longer seemed to hear her prayers, conflict with a roommate, and questions of vocational direction. When the pastor asked her what she wanted to make their focus, she said she couldn't decide, as these four areas were all equally important. She also expressed concern about the limit of five sessions and said she did not think she could get the help she needed in such a short time. Her pastor responded as follows:

Pastor: You might be right, Diane. You may need more help than I can give you. But we won't know that until we use the full five sessions. However, on the other hand, you may be quite surprised by how much help you can get once we are able to focus on one particular aspect of your life. I know it seems that they are all equally important, but perhaps you should take some time to reflect prayerfully on them. You don't need to decide today. We can end now and finish this first session next week at the same time, if that would give you a chance to think about what is most important for you right now.

Diane: Well, when you put it that way, I guess if I have to focus on one thing it would be my feeling that God has abandoned me. Maybe if I felt better about my relationship with God I might feel better about my relationship with my parents and my roommate. But does this mean that all we talk about is God?

Pastor: No. Not at all. But if your relationship with God has changed in some important ways and if that is a concern for you, let's start with that and see where it leads us. If we decide to shift our focus, we can do so, but it is still better to agree on a starting place. Why don't you use some time now to tell me more about what has changed and what you want to be different.

Commentary: Over the next several sessions, Diane continued to have trouble maintaining a focus, and her pastor had to work harder than is often the case to keep her on track. In exploring her relationship with God, they repeatedly touched on other relationships—often by way of comparison with what she was seeking from God. But her relationship with God did, in fact, provide the central organizing thread for the four sessions of their work together. Diane agreed with the pastor at the end of the last session that she had received more than she had hoped for and all she wished for at the present time.

The Engagement Stage

The second stage of strategic pastoral counseling involves the engagement of the pastor and the person seeking help around the problems that brought them together. This is the heart of the counseling process.

The term *engagement* emphasizes the fact that the pastor is now deeply involved with the person in working on these problems. Genuinely Christian counseling can never be mere advice offered from the sidelines. Pastoral counseling is always incarnational; that is, the pastor comes to the one seeking help and makes himself or herself available to be used, even sometimes abused, in the process.[4] Counseling is not only personal but also costly to the pastor. But if safety is sought by remaining on the sidelines or somehow hiding in objectivity, little help is communicated.

It is important to note that the work of this stage may well begin in the first session. The model should not be interpreted in a rigid or mechanical manner. If the goals of the first stage are completed with time remaining in the first session, the pastor can begin the tasks of the next stage. However, once the tasks of stage 1 are completed, those associated with stage 2 become the central focus.

There are two major tasks of the engagement stage: (1) the exploration of the person's feelings, thoughts, and behavioral patterns associated with the central concern, and (2) the development of new perspectives and strategies for coping or change. By now the pastor and the parishioner are hard at work on the parishioner's problems. Whereas in the first stage they could be pictured facing each other and establishing a trusting relationship, in the second stage they are standing side by side, facing the concerns brought by the person seeking help. The pastor comes alongside the person in much the same manner as is conveyed by the New Testament Greek noun *paraklēsis*. This word, in either its noun or verb forms, suggests the action of coming alongside someone to give support. God himself is pictured as "the God of all coming alongside" (2 Cor. 1:3, author's translation) or, as more commonly translated, "the God of all comfort." This is the model of the pastoral counselor.

4. See Benner (1983) for an elaboration of this incarnational view of counseling.

Although the person's feelings, thoughts, and behaviors are usually intertwined, a selective focus on each—one at a time—ensures that each is adequately addressed. Such a method also ensures that all the crucial dynamics of the person's psychospiritual functioning are considered. Because feelings, thoughts, and behaviors are intimately connected to one another, the starting point may seem somewhat arbitrary. However, an exploration of feelings is usually the best place to begin, and this should generally be followed respectively by an examination of the thoughts and behaviors associated with the feelings.

Exploring Feelings

The reason for beginning with feelings is that this is where most people normally begin when meeting with a counselor. A pastor normally first encounters in the one seeking help feelings such as anger, confusion, fear, hurt, anxiety, apathy, or depression. These feelings are often quite confusing to a pastor, and their strength or persistence may be perplexing and worrisome. Because of this, a pastor's natural reaction may be to avoid focusing on these feelings.

Another reason that pastors sometimes avoid an exploration of feelings is that the person may already seem somewhat emotionally overwhelmed, and avoiding feelings—at least temporarily—may be seen as the charitable thing to do. But feelings that are avoided are empowered. An exploration of whatever is being experienced is always preferable to reinforcing the tendency to avoid whatever is unpleasant. Consequently, an exploration of feelings is almost always the best beginning point.

Some pastoral counselors minimize the exploration of feelings in their counseling as a reaction to what they perceive to be an overemphasis on feelings in psychology—at least the popular psychology with which they may be familiar. They may have read about people who urge us to trust our emotions as a guide to what we should do or to give our emotions free expression. But in recoiling from this culture of emotionality, they have often overreacted.

The reason for this often seems to lie in a failure to understand the theology and psychology of emotions. A correct understanding of emotions must begin with the creation account presented in Scripture. God created human persons in his image and pronounced that the result was good. Emotionality was part of this original good creation, not a consequence of the fall. This means that emotionality is part of God, a point that is made abundantly clear in Scripture. God is described as experiencing sorrow (Gen. 6:5–6), anger (Deut. 13:17), pleasure (Ps. 149:4), and a great number of other emotions. Jesus also experienced grief (John 11:35), joy (John 15:11), sadness (Luke 19:41–42), and love (John 14:31). In fact, emotions were so characteristic of our Lord that he was called the Man of Sorrows.

Emotions, as all other aspects of personality, bear the effects of sin. This means that in themselves they are no more trustworthy a guide to behavior than reason or any other aspect of our nature. Expressions of emotion can be either God-honoring or sinful. But concern about the latter cannot be an excuse for repressing emotions. In fact, such emotional repression is not only the cause of many psychological problems but should also be seen as sinful in that it violates the creation design and order. Emotions were given to enrich life and energize behavior. They are intended as a catalyst for action. While we cannot simply do anything we feel like doing, we must pay attention to emotions if we are to be whole. Only when emotions are known and owned can the appropriate response to them be made.

It is strange that emotional repression often characterizes Christians. Jesus was more emotional than many contemporary conservative Christians, and in this, he was also a model of psychological maturity and health. Among the world religions, Christianity alone provides a healthy view of emotions. In contrast to the Stoics, who viewed emotions as irrational, and the Epicureans, who acquiesced to the inevitability of emotions, Jesus provides a balanced model of emotional expression. Furthermore, the Bible both affirms emotional expression (consider, for example, the Psalms) and speaks to and through our emotions. When read with the heart, not simply the mind, the Bible can be seen as emotional literature—filled with emotional expression designed to address not just our rationality but also our feelings.

The goal of the strategic pastoral counselor is to listen empathically to the feelings of the one seeking help, not to change his or her feelings. Feelings have to be faced and even expressed in order to be known. They cannot be eliminated by denying their existence. Reality can be dealt with only by facing it head-on. If feelings are to be subsequently modified, they must first be accepted in whatever form they present themselves.

The strategic pastoral counselor does not, therefore, prejudge feelings and encourage facing and accepting only those that are deemed acceptable. Feelings are simply a part of experience; they are a given. A person may not want to hate God, fear his father, or mistrust his son, but it is with this hatred, fear, or mistrust that the person must start. If the pastor is to be of help, he or she must start there too. Once feelings are accepted and owned, then the person is in a much better place to decide how to respond to them.

A final reason for encouraging a person to express his or her feelings is so that the burden may be shared. The pastor's empathic posture means that the confusion, hurt, or other disruptive feelings are held and in some cases absorbed by the pastor. This is what is meant to bear one another's burdens (Gal. 6:2). The sharing of burdens involves a mysterious redistribution of the load, and this is a central component of strategic pastoral counseling.

Exploring Thoughts

After exploring the feelings being experienced by the person seeking help, the next task is to examine the thoughts underlying those feelings. The rise of cognitive and cognitive-behavioral approaches to counseling in the last several decades has

91

done much to demonstrate the important place that faulty thinking has in causing and perpetuating problems.

A number of Christian counselors have made the exploration and modification of erroneous and unbiblical beliefs their central plank (Tan 1999; Propst 1988; Tan and Ortberg 1995). In a manner comparable to their secular counterparts, these cognitive approaches to Christian counseling emphasize that it is not so much what happens to us that makes us what we are but how we view these experiences and what we believe about ourselves and life. Thus, for example, a person is not depressed because his wife criticized him but because he has placed an inappropriate priority on being above criticism. This thought will also predispose him to anger toward his wife. But underlying both emotions—according to this cognitive perspective—is a faulty belief and an unbiblical value.

This is unquestionably often true, and it is for this reason that underlying beliefs and values must be explored in pastoral counseling. However, strategic pastoral counseling makes no assumption that these thoughts, values, and beliefs are more important than feelings. There is no reason to argue over which of the wings of an airplane is more important. Both are essential. Similarly, there is no reason to argue over whether feelings or thoughts are more important in counseling. Both are important; therefore, it is essential that the strategic pastoral counselor address both.

But whereas cognitively oriented counselors tend to emphasize the identification and correction of "wrong" thoughts and beliefs (e.g., about such things as the basis of personal worth or the source of happiness), they often fail to pay sufficient attention to another equally important cognitive task—namely, facilitating the development of an alternate perspective on one's situation. Many problems faced by people seen by pastoral counselors involve situations that cannot be changed. In such cases, this second task does not involve correcting wrong thoughts as much as developing new ways to understand those situations. This is what it means to speak of a pastoral counselor as one who brings Christian meaning to the problems experienced by those whom he or she helps (Clebsch and Jaekle 1964, 5). The new perspective that enters a situation of suffering when a person recognizes the possibility of meeting the Suffering Savior in the midst of that pain is profoundly therapeutic. And this is just what we as Christians are promised—not relief from the struggles of life but the presence of our Lord in their midst.

The development of a new understanding of a problem involves a form of teaching, but this teaching is much different from that done in a classroom. It is a gentle presentation of new ideas and an encouragement of the adoption of a new frame of reference. In this phase of strategic pastoral counseling, the explicit use of Scripture is usually most appropriate. Bearing in mind the potential misuses and problems that can be associated with such use of religious resources, the pastoral counselor should be, nonetheless, open to a direct presentation of scriptural truths when offering a new and helpful perspective on a person's situation.

The process of helping someone move toward forgiveness provides a good illustration of the way in which the development of a new understanding forms an important part of the work of strategic pastoral counseling. People who are stuck in their anger at those who have hurt them are stuck with understandings of the hurtful situation that need to be reexamined and changed. Their damaged emotions tend to distort how they perceive both the one who hurt them and themselves. In their woundedness, their perceptions are shaped by their feelings. For healing to occur, they must see themselves, the one who hurt them, and the entire hurtful event in a new light. Then and only then is healing possible.

The essence of the reinterpretation of hurt that is necessary for emotional healing is seeing the person who caused the hurt as separate from what he or she did and seeing oneself as more than one's wound. When one sees the other person as broken and needy, coping as best as they can with their own hurts and limitations, one begins to feel the first thawing of hate. Hate becomes intermixed with compassion, and this reflects the beginning movement toward the point at which one can pray for the other person. When one sees oneself as more than wounds—understanding that one also hurts others when acting out of brokenness, need, and woundedness—one is then able to identify with the person who caused the hurt. This is something that a person will initially resist, but it is essential and the core of the hard work of forgiveness. And helping others to be open to new ways of understanding their emotional wounds is the core of forgiveness counseling.

Exploring Behavior

The final task of the engagement stage of strategic pastoral counseling involves the exploration of a person's behavior. The pastor examines what the person is doing in the face of the problem and together, with the parishioner, begins to identify changes in behavior that may be desirable. For example, the parishioner may report that because of an unsatisfying marriage, he is involved in an affair; another, as a way of dealing with the news of a terminal illness, may be withdrawing from everyone around her. In reality, a person's response to such situations will always be more complex than this, and an exploration of the variety of ways in which a person has responded to an experience will be the starting point for identifying behaviors that need to be changed.

It is important that the pastor resists the temptation simply to tell the parishioner what needs to be changed. This is a main difference between counseling and preaching. Counseling involves an exploration of behavior and the sources of resistance to change, not simply telling a person what he or she must change. The parishioner must desire and own the behavioral goals. Therefore, it is most appropriate for the one seeking help to identify the goals.

A helpful way of moving toward the identification of goals is to ask the person how he or she feels about a particular behavior. Is he comfortable with his infidelity? Is she content with her withdrawal from her friends? If not, then this is the basis for a goal. If, on the other hand, the person does not wish to make any changes in the area of concern, then any goal regarding change will be the pastor's and not the parishioner's. In such a situation, it is best to avoid a direct challenge or confrontation, although the pastor should not be afraid to raise moral perspectives as long as they are not introduced in an authoritarian or moralistic manner.

The aims of this phase of strategic pastoral counseling are to identify changes that both the pastor and the parishioner agree are important and to begin to establish concrete strategies for making these changes. These tasks require wisdom, a requirement that should make the pastor keenly aware of his or her dependence on the Holy Spirit for guidance.

When working with an individual at this point in the counseling process, I pray that I will see something of what God is doing in the person's life and thereby will be better able to discern the primary areas that require change. I want to work with God in this process. I do not want to go off on a crusade of my own, attempting to make changes that merely strike me as important. I often find that prayerful attention to both what God seems to be doing in the person's life and what he seems to be leading me to do is a humbling experience. My agenda for change often does not line up well with what I believe God is suggesting. Nowhere in the entire counseling process am I more aware of my need for divine help, and that help is always available to the pastoral counselor.

After identifying areas in which changes are desirable and necessary, the pastor and the parishioner can proceed to examine the payoffs of the undesirable behavior. Rather than assuming that change will be easy, a pastor should assume that the one seeking help is getting something out of his or her present behavior. If this is true, the chances of a change occurring will be greatly enhanced if the person counts the costs associated with giving up the behavior rather than attempting to ignore those costs.

Alcohol abuse may be a means of escape, a boost to faltering self-esteem, or a source of empowerment. Minimizing what the person gets from such abuse greatly decreases the chances of significant changes being made. Similarly, withdrawal from friends may enhance a person's feelings of self-pity, or an extramarital affair may be a way of punishing a spouse. There is no simple formula for evaluating the payoffs of a specific behavior, but the importance of exploring personal meanings and payoffs of behavior cannot be overemphasized.

Behavioral goals must also be both concrete[5] and realistic. Rather than setting a goal of spending more time with friends, for example, a person might decide to contact at least two friends within the next week and try to spend time with at least one of them. Additionally, the person could name several friends whom he or she will contact. This further concretizes the plan and greatly increases the chances of its success.

Making realistic goals means that they are attainable. It also usually means that they are incremental, that is, they move a person forward in small steps rather than in one giant and likely unsuccessful step. For example, a father who wants to be more involved with his son should probably not start with the goal of taking his son on an extended father-son camping trip. Rather, a series of smaller activities that allow him to reintroduce himself into his son's life in a more gradual manner will likely be much more successful.

The key to the engagement stage of the counseling process is the pastor and the parishioner working together on the problem they identified as the central concern. Strategic pastoral counseling does not require pastors to be experts who listen to problems and then solve them. Rather, it requires that they serve as fellow pilgrims who join in the journey for a short time and who, by sharing the load, provide help for the continuing journey. And it is hoped that, as happened to the disciples who walked the Emmaus road with their unrecognized Master, the meeting will aid in opening parishioners' eyes to God, who is at work in the midst of their life circumstances and is with them on their journey. The true Counselor is, of course, God, who is the source of all life and all healing. This awareness should be a great comfort to both those seeking help and pastoral counselors.

5. The requirement that these goals be concrete contrasts with the earlier described general goals that guide the entire counseling process. There it was noted that the overall goals do not need to describe specific behavioral outcomes. However, the establishment of concrete behavioral goals is an important part of the focus on behavior that is required at this stage of strategic pastoral counseling.

The Disengagement Stage

Ending a counseling relationship should be made easier by recognizing that pastoral counseling is not the encounter and engagement simply of two people but of two people with God. The God who is present in the moments of deepest pain, confusion, and despair is a God who does not depart at the end of the fifth session. He will continue to be present as the parishioner goes on with life. But the counseling sessions do need to end, and the last stage of work together involves preparation for this event.

Evaluating Progress and Assessing Remaining Concerns

The evaluation of progress is usually a process that both pastor and parishioner will find rewarding. Some evaluating may be done in earlier sessions, but it is still a good idea to use the last session to undertake a brief review of what has been learned from the experience. Closely associated with this evaluation, of course, is an identification of remaining concerns. Seldom is everything resolved after five or fewer sessions. This means that the parishioner is preparing to leave counseling with some work yet to be done. But he or she does so with goals and plans for the future, and the development of these is an important task of the disengagement stage of strategic pastoral counseling.

As mentioned earlier, it is often advisable to take a break of several weeks before the final session. The parishioner can then work on the goals set in the engagement stage, returning for a concluding session to evaluate progress, reflect on the experience, and adjust (if necessary) goals and strategies. The final session should also include an identification of difficulties that may be encountered in the future and a consideration of ways to deal with them. Role play or other forms of behavioral rehearsal are often helpful at this stage, particularly if the person is dealing with a difficult interpersonal situation.

Arranging a Referral

If significant problems remain, the last session should also be used to make referral arrangements. Ideally, such arrangements should be discussed in earlier sessions. It might even be helpful for the parishioner to meet with the new counselor before the last session of strategic pastoral counseling. The pastor and the parishioner could, therefore, process the experience as part of the final pastoral counseling session.

Recognition of one's limitations of time, experience, training, and ability is an indispensable component of the practice of any professional. This is particularly important for counselors, since no counselor is able to help everyone who seeks his or her help. Furthermore, even if a counselor is able to provide some help, often supplementary forms of help are required. The need to refer to others does not, therefore, suggest inadequacy on a counselor's part. Rather, it suggests that the counselor is aware of his or her limits and is functioning appropriately within them.

Pastors need to be aware of the resources within their communities and prepared to refer parishioners for help that they can better receive elsewhere. This help may take the form of financial counseling, tax advice, legal counsel, or medical or psychological consultation, assessment, and treatment. Often the help that is needed is available through a community social service agency. While such resources are often rather limited in rural and smaller urban centers, most large metropolitan areas have an abundance of professional services in these areas.

Referrals to physicians (including psychiatrists) and psychologists are often particularly difficult and deserve special consideration. The family doctor should, in general, be the point of first contact regarding medical or psychiatric problems. If the person is run down physically or is experiencing significant weight loss or gain, disruptions of normal sleeping patterns, pronounced changes in sexual interest, or any other medical symptoms, he or she should be encouraged to consult a family physician as soon as possible.

The same is true with regard to the presence of a major psychiatric illness. If a person is experiencing delusions (false beliefs held despite evidence to the contrary [e.g., believing one is Jesus Christ]) or hallucinations (perceptions that occur in the absence of a corresponding sensory experience [e.g., hearing voices when none are present] or that dramatically distort or alter experience [e.g., hearing personal messages in the static on the radio]), a pastor should refer him or her to a family physician or a psychiatrist with whom the pastor has a working relationship.

The same action is appropriate if the person suffers from serious depression (lasting longer than one month and involving substantial alteration of behavior) or displays manic behavior (elevated mood that manifests itself in inappropriate euphoria and exuberance, an inflated sense of well-being, increased motor behavior and energy level that may be exhibited in boisterous and pressured speech, hyperactivity, flight of ideas, or impulsive and irrational behavior). These are some of the main symptoms of schizophrenia, bipolar disorder, and paranoid disorder. Pastoral counselors should be sufficiently familiar with these disorders and their symptoms so as to recognize them when they are encountered.

Organic mental disorders also require a medical referral. These include the consequences of substance abuse (such as alcohol organic mental disorder) as well as psychological or behavioral abnormality associated with brain disease or dysfunction (delirium, dementia, amnesic syndrome, organic personality syndrome, and organic affective syndrome). Persons evidencing long-term chronic substance abuse should also be referred to a physician.

People suffering from these and other serious mental disorders may still need and benefit from strategic pastoral counseling. The need for a referral does not mean that the pastor has nothing to give such an individual. Rather, it means that the pastor does not have all that such an individual needs. Neither does a physician, however, and this is why it is important not to discount the contribution that a pastoral counselor can make to an individual who is mentally ill. These major mental illnesses are all rooted in faulty physiology and are all appropriately treated with drugs that address the underlying physical problems. To fail to refer for medical care is irresponsible. However, while the sources of these problems lie in bodily processes, their effects reach into psychological and spiritual aspects of life. There is much that pastors can give such people if they can get past their fear and recognize the mentally ill to be persons like themselves who struggle with things beyond their control.

Various other mental and psychological disorders also usually require referral to a mental health professional but do not generally require medical intervention. Sexual disorders (exhibitionism, pedophilia, transsexualism, transvestism, and voyeurism), sexual dysfunctions (inhibited sexual desire, excitement, or orgasm), anxiety and affective disorders (depression, obsessive-compulsive disorder, phobias, panic disorders, and general anxiety disorders), personality disorders (borderline personality disorder, antisocial personality disorder, compulsive personality disorder, histrionic personality disorder, narcissistic personality disorder, and schizoid personality disorder), and dissociative disorders (fugue disorder, multiple personality disorder, and psychogenic amnesia) are appropriately treated by more intensive forms of psychotherapy than most pastors are trained to provide and normally warrant a referral to a psychologist or other qualified psychotherapist.

Finally, many marital and family problems require the specialized intervention of a qualified marital and family therapist. Pastors should not assume that they are appropriately qualified to treat all such relational problems. Entrenched patterns of marital or family pathology are seldom changed rapidly, and their treatment is a specialized form of work that not even all psychologists, psychiatrists, or social workers can provide. Persons who identify themselves as marital and family therapists, particularly if they hold qualifications in a nationally recognized association such as the American Association of Marital and Family Therapists, can usually provide the necessary help and should be consulted when serious patterns of family dysfunction exist and resist change.

Experiences with non-Christian therapists who have a religious axe to grind have made many pastors understandably anxious about referring a parishioner to someone who may not be a Christian. But often a pastor's referral options are quite limited. In these cases, a referral to someone who is competent in intensive psychotherapy but who is not a Christian can be complemented by a relationship of spiritual guidance with someone in the congregation who is recognized for his or her spiritual maturity. This relationship is not a counseling relationship. Its aim is not to explore problems and develop solutions that enhance growth. Rather, the purpose of this relationship is prayerful examination of the spiritual implications of the therapy experience and support of the person through this experience. These meetings need not be weekly, nor do they need to be scheduled or conducted as counseling sessions normally are. But they can provide support and an ongoing spiritual watch that makes referral to a non-Christian psychotherapist a responsible option.

Preparing a parishioner for a referral is an important part of the referral process. Often people resist referral to someone else and try to manipulate a pastor into continuing the counseling relationship. They will relate past bad experiences with similar people and will beg the pastor to provide them with the help they need. While such pleas are hard to ignore because of the flattery that often accompanies them, they are accepted with great peril. Referral to others is always a serious matter, and a pastor should know referral sources and, if at all possible, refer parishioners to those in whom he or she has confidence. Failure to make a referral in spite of the presence of problems that go beyond the pastor's sphere of competence displays arrogance and folly.

Terminating Counseling

In the vast majority of cases, the termination of a strategic pastoral counseling relationship goes smoothly. Most often, both pastor and parishioner agree that there is no further need to meet, and even if they feel some sadness about the decision to discontinue counseling sessions, they know it is the right thing to do.

However, there may be times when this process is some-what difficult. As already indicated, this may be due to a parishioner's desire to continue to meet. If the sessions were helpful, and occasionally even if they were not, the parishioner may not want to terminate the relationship. He or she may have experienced a kind of acceptance or even emotional intimacy in the counseling experience that is rare or not present in the rest of life. These kinds of feelings are often at the root of dependencies that can develop within even as few as two or three counseling sessions. However, gratification of these needs and wishes is not the best way to help the person. Rather, he or she should be gently directed toward relationships in which these needs can be more appropriately met, and the limits set at the beginning of the counseling relationship should be enforced.

At other times, the difficulty in terminating will reside with the pastor. The sessions may, for any number of reasons, have been particularly enjoyable or rewarding, and this might make the pastor tempted to continue them. But once again, the best course of action is to follow through on the initial limits agreed upon by both parties.

The exception to this rule is a situation in which a parishioner is facing a significant crisis at the end of the five sessions, and there are no other available resources to provide the necessary support. If this is the case, the addition of a few sessions may be appropriate. However, the additional counseling should again be time-limited and should take the form of crisis management. It should not involve more sessions than are absolutely necessary to restore a degree of stability to the parishioner's functioning or to introduce him or her to other people who can be of assistance.

Pastoral counselors are in a unique position to help large numbers of people who will never go to any other counselor. They are also in a unique position to help many who may need further help but who choose to first consult a pastor. In the course of a typical week, pastors regularly encounter more people than most other helping professionals encounter in months, and a significant percentage of these people desperately need the help of a skilled counselor. Many of those in need will see their minister as a competent, trusted shepherd and will ask him or her to walk with them through their struggles, pain, or confusion. But as noted by Clinebell, "If the pastor lacks the required skills, such persons receive a stone when they ask for bread" (Clinebell 1984, 47).

Strategic pastoral counseling provides a framework for pastors who seek to counsel in a way that is congruent with the rest of their pastoral responsibilities and that is psychologically informed and responsible. While skill in implementing the model comes only with time, it is quite possible for most pastors to acquire that skill. However, counseling skills cannot be adequately learned simply by reading books. As with all interpersonal skills, they must be learned through practice, and, ideally, this practice is best acquired in a context of supervisory feedback from a more experienced pastoral counselor.

The pastor who has mastered these skills is in a position to proclaim the Word of God in a highly personalized and relevant manner to people who are often desperate for help. This is a unique and richly rewarding opportunity. Rather than scattering seed in a broadcast manner across ground that is often stony and hard, the pastoral counselor has the opportunity to plant one seed at a time. Knowing the soil conditions, he or she is also able to plant in a highly individualized manner, taking pains to ensure that a seed will not be quickly blown away, and then gently to water and nourish its growth. This is the unique opportunity for the ministry of pastoral counseling. It is my prayer that pastors will see the centrality of counseling to their call to ministry, feel encouraged by an approach to pastoral counseling that lies within the skills and availability of most pastors, and will accept these responsibilities with renewed vigor and clarity of direction.

Additional Readings

Benner, D., and R. Harvey. 1996. *Understanding and facilitating forgiveness.* Grand Rapids: Baker. This book presents an application of strategic pastoral counseling to problems of forgiveness, providing particularly helpful case illustrations of the interaction of the work of emotional exploration and the development of new understandings in the process of forgiveness counseling.

Benner, D., and P. Hill, eds. 1999. *Baker encyclopedia of psychology and counseling.* 2d ed. Grand Rapids: Baker. This twelve-hundred-page encyclopedia presents the symptoms and current recommended treatments for 184 mental disorders. It is also a good general resource for a Christian perspective on a wide variety of topics in psychology.

Egan, G. 2001. *The skilled helper.* 7th ed. Belmont, Calif.: Wadsworth. This book, not written specifically for pastors but for anyone seeking to learn the basics of counseling, contains excellent overviews of stages of the counseling process and the major tasks of the counselor in each. It also contains an abundance of practical information about the conduct of the counseling interview and basic counseling strategies and techniques.

Malony, H. N. 1988. The clinical assessment of optimal religious functioning. *Review of Religious Research* 30, no. 1:2–17. This is the primary source of the religious status interview described in this chapter. The article contains the interview questions as well as a discussion of the development of the instrument and some of the research up to 1988 on its applications.

Miller, W., and K. Jackson. 1985. *Practical psychology for pastors.* Englewood Cliffs, N.J.: Prentice-Hall. This practical handbook of psychology for pastors contains a good discussion of the major mental disorders. The stages of counseling described do not exactly overlap those proposed in strategic pastoral counseling, but the discussion of counseling stages is helpful.

Tan, S. Y. 1999. Cognitive-behavior therapy. In *Baker encyclopedia of psychology and counseling,* edited by D. Benner and P. Hill. 2d ed. Grand Rapids: Baker. A helpful overview of the cognitive approach to counseling, including guidelines for conducting a distinctively Christian approach to such counseling.

Tan, S. Y., and J. Ortberg. 1995. *Understanding depression.* Grand Rapids: Baker. This book presents an application of strategic pastoral counseling to the treatment of depression and is a good illustration of the work of exploring the underlying thoughts that frequently lie behind depression.

Wicks, R., R. Parsons, and D. Capps, eds. 1985. *Clinical handbook of pastoral counseling.* New York: Paulist Press. This volume provides a remarkably rich resource for pastoral counselors who are not troubled by the broader ecumenical perspective of many of the contributors. Built around thirty-one chapters that present a variety of perspectives on pastoral counseling and applications of it to special populations, it offers help for the beginner and seasoned pastoral counselor alike.

5

Ellen: A Five-Session
Case Illustration

To illustrate the principles outlined in the previous chapters, this chapter presents a case study of an individual seen by a strategic pastoral counselor. Ellen was a thirty-one-year-old woman who contacted a pastor by phone and asked if she could come to see him. The pastor knew her only slightly, as she and her husband were new to the congregation. He had spoken to them both after their first Sunday at the church and had noticed Ellen present several times since then, although not with her husband.

In that first contact, Ellen had done most of the talking. She indicated that they had recently moved to the city because of her husband's job transfer. The pastor sensed some conflict between them in this brief encounter and also thought Ellen seemed somewhat agitated. This was all that he knew of her at the point of the phone call.

That call gave little additional information. Her voice betrayed no unusual distress, and she did not give any indication of the nature of her concerns. She did, however, betray a mild degree of urgency when she stated that she hoped he would be able to see her within the next few days. She also indicated that she would make herself available at any time to accommodate his schedule. An appointment was set for 9 A.M. at the church office the next morning.

Commentary: Before the first counseling session, most pastors know something about the person they are going to see. Even in Ellen's case, the pastor has had more direct contact with her than is usually the case with someone consulting a psychotherapist. Additional information is usually also given in the conversation when the parishioner requests a counseling session. The strategic pastoral counselor weighs all this information carefully, not to prejudge the situation or attempt to anticipate what will transpire in the first session but rather to ensure that all the available information is being marshaled in the attempt, which begins even at this point, to get to know the person seeking help.

It is also worth commenting on the conduct of the conversation in which the request for a consultation is made. This ought to be kept brief. All that needs to be done is to indicate one's availability (or unavailability) and, assuming the former, establish a time and place for the first meeting. The length of the first session should also be communicated. It is usually not appropriate to ask questions about the nature of the concerns or to encourage the person to talk about them at this point. In fact, it is more appropriate to say to the parishioner who begins to talk about his or her problems that there is no need to say more now but that one looks forward to hearing about these concerns in detail at the first session. Someone in crisis is obviously an exception to this general principle.

First Session

Ellen arrived for the first appointment ten minutes early. After inviting her into his office, the pastor stated that he was glad to see her and invited her to share with him whatever it was that had brought her to him at this time.

Ellen began by stating that she hoped she was not imposing on his time and apologized for calling the church since she was not a member and had only attended on a few occasions. She then said it was very important for her to talk to a pastor and that the reason for this would become apparent quickly. In a few sentences, she then laid out the core of her present distress. She had recently had an abortion and was experiencing considerable guilt over it. This was, however, only the beginning of her problems. She had discovered two days prior to calling the pastor that complications from the abortion would require a partial hysterectomy and that she would never be able to have children. She then went on to speak of the anger she felt toward her husband, whom she said had talked her into the abortion. This anger was mixed with sadness over the loss of childbearing capacity and guilt over her own complicity in the abortion. She cried for much of the time while relaying this information.

Commentary: This part of the session lasted roughly ten minutes, and during it the pastor said very little. Ellen looked up at him through her tears on several occasions and seemed comforted that he was obviously deeply attentive and warmly present. Had he sensed that she needed more verbal input from him, it would have been quite appropriate to offer measured support by saying something like, "I'm sure that must have been very distressing for you" or "I sense how disappointing that news must have been." These minimalist interventions would demonstrate sensitivity to her emotions and would encourage her to continue to express them. Often, however, the same thing can be communicated nonverbally. The crucial matter is that the parishioner knows that the pastor is listening and is accepting of her feelings. There are, however, as many ways in which this can be communicated as there are counselors.

It is also important to note that the pastor felt no need to try to make Ellen feel better (or, if such a need was present, he did not gratify it). Reassurances would have merely temporarily suppressed her feelings and might have moved her away from them. Expressions of sympathy ("I'm really very sorry to hear that") would have been irrelevant and would have moved her from a focus on her feelings toward a focus on the feelings of the pastor. However, the pastor's empathy let her know that he was listening and was open to trying to understand her feelings. Sympathy is more of a psychological hand-on-a-shoulder, and while it has its place, it is generally therapeutically inferior to empathy. In Ellen's case, there would be a time to try to help her feel better, but it was not yet that time. Before she could move away from her intense and painful feelings, she needed to experience and express them.

At the end of this outpouring of feelings, Ellen looked directly at the pastor and the following interchange occurred:

Ellen: You must think me an awful person for what I have done. I have violated everything that I always believed in and am not sure I can ever forgive myself. I do know that I can never expect God to forgive me.

Pastor: In fact, I don't think you are an awful person. But what strikes me is how awful you feel. You have obviously failed yourself and feel you have failed God. It seems that you feel so bad about this that you think you don't deserve ever to be forgiven.

Commentary: This was an excellent intervention. The pastor wisely gave a brief response to Ellen's request for information about how he was feeling about her but then quickly moved back to the issues and feelings at hand. Ellen was beginning to move toward a discussion of her feelings about herself and God, and this was very important. By his response, the pastor reminded her of this direction and encouraged her to continue.

Ellen: That's for sure! I have failed myself. I can't believe I actually had an abortion. I have always been pro-life. In fact, at university I even marched in pro-life rallies. My friends would be disgusted with me if they knew what I have done. But most of all I keep thinking about

how I have failed God. He is the one who must really
be disgusted with me.

Pastor: Who is this God you have failed?

Commentary: This brief intervention illustrates a timely
and appropriate giving of direction on the part of the pastor.
By this, he encouraged Ellen to explore further the spiritual
aspects of the situation, matters to which she had alluded
twice.

Ellen: The same as your God. I'm a Christian.

Pastor: Yes, but tell me more about how you experience this
God. What is he like? How do you relate to him and
he to you? I'm interested in knowing a bit more about
how God fits into your life and what difference being
a Christian makes for you.

Ellen then proceeded to describe a God who was experienced entirely in terms of law with almost no appreciation
whatsoever of grace. In response to a question from the pastor
as to whether or not there was any place for forgiveness in the
way this God deals with Christians, she said that while she
knew that Christians were supposed to believe this, it was not
something she knew much about from personal experience.
She also indicated that she had prayed for forgiveness but
had not felt any better after doing so. This led to the following exchange:

Pastor: I believe that for us humans, giving and receiving
forgiveness is a process. Only God can do it instantly.
Feelings are involved in this process, but they are not
the whole matter. We will come back to this and will
work together on the question as to why you are stuck
in this process. But first I'd like to hear a bit more about
how you relate to this God who has such high standards,
standards that you find quite impossible to meet.

Ellen: That's my feeling exactly. It's fine for God to set the
rules. He can keep them easily. He's God. But I'm only

human. God doesn't live with my husband. As far as I know, he doesn't even have a career, and he certainly doesn't face the kinds of pressures I do to keep my marriage together, develop my career, and still try to be a good Christian. I know God disapproves of what I have done. But it's easy for him.

Pastor: I'm not so sure I agree that it's easy for God to see you struggle and have such a hard time doing what you know you should do. I don't even think that he looks at you and simply feels disgust and anger. Everything that I know about our God indicates that he closely identifies with us. That's what the incarnation is all about. I don't believe he turns his back and walks away from you when you fail him. But do you have any sense that what I say is true?

Ellen: I would like to believe that. I really would. But I don't sense God with me, especially not now.

Commentary: The pastor's interventions through this section of the session clearly illustrate the way in which counseling can serve a proclamatory role. He first introduced the good news indirectly by means of a question ("I wonder if there is any place for forgiveness in the way this God deals with his people?") and then more directly shared his belief that God is with and for his people. But unlike preaching, all of this was done within the context of dialogue.

While much of what the pastor said in this section had an educative or didactic quality, it was balanced by considerable sensitivity to Ellen's feelings. The pastor also continued to relate primarily to her experience. After a brief statement about the meaning of the incarnation, he checked to see if she found this believable or helpful and, in so doing, kept close to her experience.

Pastor: Was there a time when you felt more like God was with and for you?

Commentary: This question moved Ellen toward the broader context for her present problem. The pastor took the first step in moving her toward a history of her spiritual and religious functioning. This was quite appropriate at this point in the session.

After a moment of thought, Ellen described several childhood memories of services in the Episcopal church in which she was reared. These were times of peace and calm, and she reported a keen sense of God's presence in the services and in herself. She indicated that in childhood her primary sense of God was that of a being of love, peace, and beauty.

When asked what brought this to an end, Ellen spoke of the radical transformation in her family that occurred when she was eleven. At that time, her parents had what they viewed to be a conversion experience. They then began to attend a small evangelical church in their community, and their family life quickly became centered in this church. Ellen described this as the end of her childhood, at least the happy childhood she had known to that point. Her parents, she said, became less fun-loving and much more rigid in the rules they laid down for her and her younger sister.

When asked to talk a bit more about her mother and father, Ellen said she had always been closer to her mother, whom she experienced as emotionally supportive, even if somewhat caught up in her own world. Her mother had been a professional musician in the early years of their family's life but was forced into an early retirement by serious health problems when Ellen was eight. Her mother was quite depressed at this time and seemed to withdraw from Ellen and the rest of the family. She felt that her mother had never really come back to her and her sister. At the point at which her health began to improve several years later, her mother shifted her emotional attachments to the new church, and Ellen said she was left feeling like an orphan.

Ellen's father was a physician and was never a very important part of her childhood. She said she never really knew him. Her most important encounters as a child with him were in his role as disciplinarian. In general, he seemed to her to be uncaring and authoritarian. She also reported that he was never satisfied with what she did, telling her that she was capable of doing better and never showing appreciation for what she did in fact accomplish. Ellen reported that she felt her relationship with her father had improved somewhat since her marriage, but he remained the object of a low level of resentment.

Next, the pastor asked Ellen if she could tell him a bit about her husband and their marriage. Ellen had met Rick at college, and they had dated off and on over the next few years before marrying when they were both twenty-five. At that time, one of the things she most appreciated about him was what she perceived to be his support for her career. This was very important to her, as she had by then defined her worth in terms of professional achievements. Viewing her mother as a failure because she had given up her career, Ellen wanted desperately to make something of herself, and Rick's support of this was very important.

Their marriage had been basically happy and seemed to have some significant strengths. Children had been the one big area of conflict. Although Ellen had had no intention of giving up her career as an interior designer, she had wanted to have children at some point. Rick had been less sure about whether he wanted children but had been very clear that it was definitely not the right time for either of them. Over time, Ellen came to feel that his concerns about children were not really concerns for her but reflected his own selfish desire not to have any distractions as he continued to climb the corporate ladder. Over the past year, they had fought about this on a number of occasions. These fights had become much more frequent since the abortion. While the abortion had certainly been at least in part a concession to her husband's pressure, Ellen had gone along with the idea because she had not planned to get pregnant and had felt it to be very bad timing for her business. Her husband seemed to have little understanding of the guilt and conflict she experienced over the abortion. She had not yet even told him about the loss of childbearing capacity.

Commentary: This exploration of her family of origin and her marriage took almost twenty minutes. The pastor noted many topics for future discussion but at this point kept Ellen on track and remained attentive. He was beginning to make connections in his own mind concerning Ellen's relationship with her father, her husband, and her God, but he refrained from commenting on them. Noting that there were just over ten minutes left before the end of the hour, he then introduced one final transition.

Pastor: Well, we are nearing the end of our time together this morning, and perhaps we should pull some of these things together and see where we are. You have covered a lot of ground, and I think I have a reasonably good sense of the concerns that brought you to me. But how are you feeling about our conversation to this point?

Ellen: I feel tremendously relieved to be able to tell you about the mess I am in. I have kept most of this to myself, and I knew I couldn't continue to do it. But I still feel stuck. I don't know how to cope with the feelings I have.

Pastor: What feelings are most upsetting?

Ellen: Well, I guess more than anything I feel guilt. But I also feel a lot of anger toward myself and my husband. And I feel unbelievably sad about the news I just got—the news that I won't ever be able to have kids of my own. I guess maybe that's God's way of punishing me for what I did.

Pastor: Once again, I'm not so sure that is the way God really works. I suspect that your idea of God contains a number of significant distortions, and I would like to look at some of those further, that is, if you want to come back and see me again.

Ellen: Oh yes. I would like to do that.

Pastor: Well, I would be very pleased to work with you some more on this. Why don't we meet the same time next week? I should tell you that I do all my counseling within a five-session limit, so that means we will have a maximum of four more sessions. However, if we can agree on a focus and if you are willing to continue to be as forthright and hardworking as you have been today, I think that will be ample time. But one thing we need to be clear on before we end today is exactly what it is you most want help with.

Ellen: That's pretty clear. My feelings. Particularly the guilt.

Pastor: It may be a bit difficult to determine right at the moment which of your feelings is most central and important. I suspect that you may find yourself moving back and forth between guilt, anger, and sadness. But I agree with you that perhaps the best place to start is with your feelings of guilt and your experience of God. If you can come to experience God's forgiveness and grant yourself and your husband that same forgiveness, I suspect you will then be in a much better position to deal with the other feelings you are facing.

Ellen: I agree. I guess that is why I came to see you. I would like to talk with you a few more times and see if you can help me sort out some of the stuff that is so jumbled up in me.

Pastor: Before we conclude, I wonder how you would feel about my praying with you.

Ellen: I would like that.

Pastor: All right, let's pray. [Brief prayer.] I also wonder if you are open to doing any reading during the week. In particular, I have a couple of passages of Scripture that I would like to have you read and reflect on. Perhaps we can begin next time by briefly discussing your reactions to them. [Ellen nods her assent.] Okay then, I would like you to read two passages of Scripture that deal with an aspect of God that I suspect is somewhat alien to your experience. One image of God that is repeated throughout the Old and New Testaments is that of the shepherd. I would like you to read John 10, where Jesus describes himself as the Good Shepherd, and Psalm 23, where David talks about experiencing God as the Good Shepherd. As you do this, take some time to meditate on Christ as the Good Shepherd. You may want to write down your thoughts about this. Next week, tell me your reactions, whatever they may be, to these passages.

Commentary: This ended the first session. In this session, the pastor was quite successful in accomplishing the goals of the first stage of counseling. He and Ellen achieved a good working alliance, she clearly identified her central concerns, and they together explored the context of these concerns. It is also worth noting that this first session contained a preview of much of the work that would follow. The exploration of Ellen's emotions was well underway, as were the cognitive tasks of exploring the beliefs that helped her interpret her experience and suggesting new understandings. An exploration of the behavioral component of her functioning was begun with a brief discussion of the abortion and her ways of relating to her husband. Together these served to introduce Ellen to the way in which counseling would work and helped her to anticipate what would occur in later sessions.

The suggestion that Ellen reflect on two passages of Scripture was not offered with the expectation that this would set her thinking straight about God. Rather, the Scripture reading was intended to point her toward the God of Scripture and to help her see how he differed from the God of her experience. Another assignment that might have helped her prepare for the next session would have been that she keep a feeling journal during the week. Directly tying the homework (if any is assigned) to the intended focus of the next session is an excellent way to help the parishioner prepare for the upcoming session.

Second Session (One Week Later)

In response to the pastor's question about how her week had gone, Ellen stated that she had felt better since their last conversation. She said that her reflection on the passages of Scripture had been quite helpful. She had quickly realized that she had never personally encountered God as a loving, caring, gentle shepherd. This led her to talk more about how she did in fact experience God. She spoke of her fear of him and her feelings of guilt. On two occasions she also said something like, "I just can't believe that I did it, that I actually had an abortion!" After the second of these, the pastor responded by saying that while she spoke of having trouble believing that God could ever forgive her, he was hearing that it was her forgiveness of herself that seemed to be more difficult. He said that her language of "kicking herself" (a phrase she had just used) suggested that her feelings of guilt in relation to God and her anger at herself were mixed together.

Commentary: The pastor's primary goal for this session was to unravel Ellen's emotions. In the opening moments, he noticed that she was confusing her feelings toward God and those toward herself. She was talking about God but was continually expressing feelings about herself. He made this observation to help her further express and explore her feelings and differentiate between related feelings.

Ellen responded to this observation by focusing on and expressing her anger at herself. She said she was not prepared to forgive herself because she did not deserve forgiveness. The pastor noted that while last week they had talked about God's standards being impossibly high, it appeared that this was also true of her own standards for herself. Ellen agreed that her standards for herself were high but said that this was basic to who she was. She went on to say that long ago she had set an agenda of being beyond reproach as a way of ensuring that she secure the respect and acceptance of those around her. This led to the following exchange:

Pastor: I think you have just expressed something of crucial importance. It sounds to me as if your problem isn't so much with God's standards as it is with your inability to keep them. Your own internalized standards seem, from what I see of them, to be not that much different from God's. But while God clearly understands that you are human and knows that in yourself you are totally incapable of keeping his law, you make no such concessions for yourself. Instead, you expect yourself to *be* God. You expect yourself to make no mistakes, to commit no sin. You demand that you be the sort of person who will never need forgiveness, either from yourself or others.

Ellen: [Beginning to cry.] That's true. I do demand that I be perfect. I guess I always have. It's what my parents seemed to expect of me, and I guess it's what I thought God expected of me. It seemed like the way to make sure I got their love. But it didn't work. I was never good enough, particularly for my father.

Pastor: How did that feel—to never measure up to your father's expectations of you?

Commentary: This illustrates good therapeutic dialogue. Ellen was exploring and expressing her feelings, and the tangled web of emotions was slowly being unraveled. One set of feelings led to another, and the pastor's acceptance of each of them reflected God's acceptance of her and modeled a way in which she would hopefully learn to accept herself.

The pastor's question illustrates an important principle when seeking to unravel emotions. The fact that Ellen's feelings were mixed up means that she had been experiencing a variety of feelings in relation to a variety of objects. The pastor's job was to move through this range of material systematically. If Ellen had been setting the direction of the session, she would have tended to flip-flop rapidly among these various feelings and objects. The pastor knew that all (or most) of them would eventually have to be explored, but he also knew that it would be best if they were explored one at a time. This could not be done in a rigid manner, however,

117

as they were closely interconnected. After focusing on her anger at herself, he suggested (following her lead) that she explore her feelings in relation to her father.

Ellen responded to this encouragement to explore her feelings about never being able to meet her father's expectations by crying. She expressed the frustration of a young girl who admired her father and longed for his affection but seemed to receive only his judgment. She felt that she never quite met his standards, even when she did her very best. Feelings of frustration and despair were intermixed with feelings of anger. Following the trail of her anger, Ellen stated that because her father was impossible to please, she had given up trying and no longer cared what he thought of her. To help Ellen maintain the focus on her feelings, the pastor ignored his inclination to question whether this was really true. Instead, he asked her whether she saw any parallels between how she felt about her father and how she felt about God. She answered that God was harder to ignore and that while she felt anger toward her father, she felt only guilt with regard to God. This led to the following exchange:

Pastor: But perhaps your trouble in believing that God still loves you even when you fall short of his standards is related to the fact that you never found this to be true of your father. And, as you say, God is harder to ignore, probably harder to be angry at. Therefore, you feel guilty about what you have done but have trouble with the idea of taking his freely offered forgiveness. You want to earn his love, not receive it as a gift. All your experiences suggest that love needs to be earned, and the idea of unconditional love makes you very uncomfortable.

Ellen: I think that is true. I am afraid to be angry at God, and I don't really want his forgiveness. I just want to feel better. But I don't want any handouts. I want to earn it. I'll do anything to feel better, but I don't deserve to have someone just let me off the hook.

Pastor: You're so bad you deserve punishment. What you have done is so awful that justice won't be done until you suffer for it. Forgiveness feels like it is too easy, too cheap.

Ellen: Yes, that is how it feels. [Crying.] I took the life of my baby because I didn't want it to interfere with my career. *I* did that. No one really made me. Sure, it was what my husband wanted me to do, but he didn't put a gun to my head. I did it. What I did was wrong. I *feel* guilty because I *am* guilty.

Pastor: I see your feelings of guilt not as a sign that God is punishing you but as a sign of mercy. They are a gift of God, an indication that he is with you. He wants to wrap you in his love and hopes, I believe, that you will meet him in the midst of your guilty feelings. You have also just accomplished confession. Remember that the Bible says, "If we confess our sins, he is faithful and just to forgive us." You have just done what God asks. The next thing is to accept what he says he will do. His forgiveness is there for the taking. You may not immediately and finally feel better about everything that has happened, but be assured, he has forgiven you.

Commentary: This comment by the pastor is a bit long. He simply tries to pack too much into one statement. However, it ends in a good place because he points her back to her feelings.

Ellen: I do want his forgiveness, but you are right. It's hard to take it because I feel that I deserve to be punished. Or at least I don't deserve to be forgiven.

Pastor: You're right not to minimize the seriousness of sin, but the good news is that someone else took your sin and punishment—Jesus. What you did was wrong. Forgiveness does not overlook that fact. But God longs to forgive you and loves you deeply, even when you sin.

Ellen: [Crying.] I've always known that, but I guess I have never really accepted it. I do want God's forgiveness. I think I am ready to take it now.

Pastor: Well, as I said before, it is now yours. Believe that. You don't need to do one more thing to be assured that God has wholly and completely forgiven you for what you have done.

Commentary: This was a very important turning point in the work with Ellen. The pastor had already told her that she should not expect all her bad feelings to suddenly and completely disappear. In both the first and second sessions, he said that her feelings were not a reliable indication of the reality of God's forgiveness. Ellen now seemed genuinely ready to claim that forgiveness, and this would turn out to be a watershed moment for her.

The second session ended shortly after this. The pastor loaned Ellen a book on guilt and forgiveness that he said would help her reflect further on some of the things they had discussed. He then suggested that in preparation for the next session, which both agreed would be two weeks later, Ellen should think more about how she was working to earn the respect and acceptance of other people. He also encouraged her to keep track of significant feelings she experienced and to record these and other thoughts in a diary, from which she could share as she chose in the next session.

Commentary: Although the intended focus of this session was the exploration and expression of feelings, the actual process of the session demonstrates how closely feelings and thoughts are interconnected. The session involved productive emotional work, but the pastor also continued the work of correcting some misconceptions about the nature of God, and Ellen seemed to genuinely experience God's forgiveness. This session was, therefore, a good illustration of the work of stage 2 of strategic pastoral counseling.

The homework assignment was the pastor's attempt to begin to connect some of the threads that he had seen emerge in the first two sessions. He sensed that Ellen's relationship with God contained significant parallels to her relationship with her father and possibly with her husband. The first session had established feelings of guilt and anger as the primary focus for the counseling relationship. In the second session, she dealt primarily with the guilt side of this focus, working particularly on her relationship with God. Her relationship with her father, however, was never far from the surface of the discussion. It was this observation that led the pastor to suggest a homework assignment that he hoped would help Ellen to begin making connections between the ways she viewed and related to her earthly father and her heavenly Father.

Third Session (Two Weeks Later)

Ellen began this session by telling the pastor that she had been quite depressed since the last session. While she had experienced less guilt and generally had felt better in relation to God, she had increasingly felt despair over the loss of her childbearing capacity, which would result from the surgery she faced within the next week. She had informed her husband about the surgery, and he seemed to be more supportive and understanding than she had expected. However, she felt stuck in this despair, now realizing more than ever how badly she had wanted one day to have her own children.

Commentary: The pastor had approached this third session with a plan to use it to explore the ways in which Ellen's relationships with her husband, family, and possibly others involved the same act of working for love and respect that they had discovered in her relationship with God. However, the first moments of this session revealed that Ellen had her own agenda. What should he do?

His decision to set his agenda aside was the correct one. The issues she was raising were intimately related to the mutually defined focus they had previously established. His plan for the session had been a reasonable one. At this stage of the counseling process, however, it was impossible to predict what feelings would emerge after a session like the preceding one. The feelings of despair she was experiencing were an intensification of her earlier feelings of sadness. This was not a new topic but a continuation of an old one. It was appropriate, therefore, for the pastor to set his plans aside and follow the direction she suggested.

This does not mean that the strategic pastoral counselor should always be prepared to let the parishioner set the agenda for a session. If Ellen had begun this session with questions regarding future directions for her business, the pastor would have been correct to remind her gently of their agreed-upon focus and to ask how this new material related to that focus. It is certainly possible to change the focus by mutual consent. However, a change of direction should always be made explicitly. If a change in focus is not made, it is the pastor's job to suggest a return to the original focus. This can be done by asking about the homework assignment.

The pastor encouraged Ellen to talk more about her desire to have her own children. He also suggested that she explore the loss her upcoming surgery represented. This led her into a long discussion of some of the things she thought having a child would give her, including a chance to love someone in a way she had not yet let herself love anyone and a chance to rear a child better than she perceived her parents to have done. She also said that although she had been disappointed with her mother for giving up her career because of her illness, she admired her for investing as much of herself as she had in her parenting role. This led Ellen back to her anger at her father. The pastor ignored this theme and instead kept her focused on the anticipated payoffs of childbearing as a way of helping her begin a process of grief work.

When asked why it was important to do a better job of rearing a child than her own parents had done, she said she didn't know. The pastor asked her to reflect on this and not to assume that it was self-evident. After some reflection, she stated that perhaps she felt this way because she had no hope of meeting her father's expectations regarding vocational success, and therefore, she wanted to beat him in the one area where it was possible to do so. She thought of another possibility: Perhaps vocational success was not as important to her as she had thought and that rearing a family was the real challenge she wanted. As she explored this latter possibility further, she realized that it was not an either/or matter. She did in fact genuinely want a career. This was not merely a response to the expectations of others. However, she also wanted to have a family and was not content to see children viewed as mere complications in the pursuit of a successful career. This reminded her too much of the way her father had viewed her and her sister, and she vowed that she would never look at children that way.

Ellen then began to discuss her relationship with her husband. She said he was emotionally insensitive, self-preoccupied, and incapable of genuine love for anyone other than himself. She doubted that she had ever really loved him and at times was not sure she wanted to continue the marriage. The pastor sensed that this was a much larger area of work than could be undertaken in a session or two and asked whether she had shared any of these feelings with her husband. She said they shouted things like this to each other when they were fighting, but they had not really communicated about anything of emotional significance in years. The pastor then asked her if she would consider telling her husband about her dissatisfaction with their marriage and suggesting to him that they consult a marriage counselor. She did not think he would respond well to this suggestion but said she would try to talk with him. The pastor encouraged her to have this talk before the next session and offered to help them find a marital counselor if they wished to see one.

Noting that they were within ten minutes of the end of the session, the pastor suggested that they briefly review the central concerns that had brought Ellen for counseling and consider where they should go in the next session. Ellen said that the feelings of guilt were no longer a concern but that she did want to talk more about the hysterectomy and its consequences. Although she was not particularly worried about the surgery, she felt that it was going to be a difficult experience emotionally and that she would probably want to use the next session to talk about it. She also indicated that she wanted to talk more about her relationship with her parents, as she continued to feel anger toward her father. She said that although she knew she should forgive him for treating her as he had, she was having trouble doing so and wanted to talk about that further.

The pastor responded by indicating that her relationship with her father might take them too far from their agreed-upon focus, namely, her feelings of guilt, anger at herself and her husband, and sadness about the hysterectomy. He suggested that they use the next session (scheduled for four weeks later) to work on matters related to her hysterectomy. They could, if she still wished, spend some time in the last session exploring her relationship with her father as well as pulling together any other loose ends. He also asked her if she would appreciate a visit during her stay in the hospital. She indicated that this would not be necessary and that she would prefer to talk to him at their next session. With this the third session ended.

Commentary: While the direction of this session had not been anticipated by the pastor, it was an appropriate use of their time together. The focus could, in fact, have been predicted. It is quite common for someone in counseling to feel much better after the first session and worse after the second. In the first session, telling one's story brings considerable relief. However, as the work of counseling gets under way, emotional pain comes closer to the surface, and people often feel worse. While Ellen felt better in terms of the guilt feelings that were her first concern, it was not surprising that one of the other problems identified in the initial session (the feelings of loss associated with the upcoming hysterectomy) had taken their place as the primary concern.

The pastor's management of the marital concerns expressed in this session also reflects good judgment. These problems were outside the boundaries of their agreed-upon focus. Even if Ellen's other concerns were all eliminated (or if by mutual agreement the marital concerns were given higher priority), these problems were significant and could not be meaningfully addressed in the remaining two sessions. The pastor's strategy of encouraging Ellen to share her feelings with her husband and of recommending marital counseling was good.

The review and refocusing in the last ten minutes of the session were also very important. These acts provided Ellen and the pastor with a clarification of their goals for the remaining sessions. The pastor's offer of a pastoral visit in the hospital was also appropriate. If she had accepted the offer, this visit would have been distinctly different from a counseling session, involving a brief conversation about her present situation but not about her loss of childbearing capacity or other matters scheduled to be topics of discussion in counseling.

Fourth Session (Four Weeks Later)

Ellen began the fourth session by talking about the physical experience of the surgery and her recuperation. She had not yet gone back to work, as she continued to feel quite weak. Emotionally, she was, as anticipated, still having a difficult time with the experience. She described herself as feeling less than fully female. She said she felt the way she had known some women to feel after a mastectomy—that she had lost a part of her femininity. She felt robbed of something that she did not deserve to lose, feeling that thirty-one was too young to have to undergo this surgery. The hysterectomy had reawakened feelings of anger at herself and at her husband for his part in encouraging the abortion.

During this discussion, Ellen also raised the question of whether she was experiencing God's punishment for the abortion. Although she had tangentially raised this previously, she now seemed quite troubled by the matter and posed the question directly to the pastor. He assured her that he did not believe this was a useful way to think about what had occurred. He suggested that God in his mercy reaches out to people to help them deal with the consequences of their sin, not to further the punitive natural effects of their actions. As an illustration, he cited God's provision of clothes of animal skins as replacements for Adam's and Eve's crude fig leaf coverings. He also suggested that a god who would punish her for

125

having an abortion by taking away her childbearing capacity would be a god who would have stripped Adam and Eve of their fig leaves in order to heighten their sense of shame, not at all like the God who came to them in their sin and guilt and acted redemptively. Ellen seemed to find comfort in this.

She then talked more about her feelings of never being able to give birth to a child. This continued to depress her. She talked about young girls getting pregnant when that was the last thing they wanted, while she, wanting to get pregnant, could never do so again. The pastor picked up on the expression "wanting to get pregnant" and asked her if that was, in fact, what she presently would wish for if it were possible. She said that paradoxically it was. While a mere four months ago she had terminated an unwanted pregnancy, she now felt that she would do almost anything to be pregnant again and would welcome it right that very moment. Ellen began to sob. After a moment or two, the pastor spoke:

Pastor: The pain you experience about not being able to have kids is very deep, and I sense that it leaves you feeling as if, in some ways, the bottom has fallen out of your world.

Ellen: It does. I know this isn't the end of everything, but I suddenly realize how much I really wanted to be a mother. It may not be the end of the world, but right now it feels like it.

Pastor: Yes, I think I understand that. And your feelings are real. But let's look more closely at your sense that you are at a dead end. Is that really true?

Ellen: Well, I'm not dead. That's true. But I can never have kids.

Pastor: That's what I'm questioning. Don't rule out adoption. You don't have to give birth physically to a child to have the experience of being a parent. The child that you rear with love need not be one that is a product of your body. Over the years I have known many couples who could not have their own children who chose to adopt and found it to be a richly satisfying response to their desire to be parents and rear a family. Don't rule this out at this point.

Ellen: I guess you might be right, although it would never be the same.

Pastor: It may not fit your preconceived idea of what parenting was to be about, but perhaps that idea was too narrow. Don't limit your options.

Commentary: This brief set of interventions was an attempt to keep Ellen's vistas open. When people feel despair, it is often a result of wearing blinders. The feelings must be accepted and validated, but at the same time, it is often possible to suggest other ways of viewing the situation that open up new possibilities.

Following this, Ellen continued to talk about the pervasive sense of sadness that she was experiencing. Sensing that this sadness was associated with losses that went beyond those already identified, the pastor asked her if she could think of anything else that she had lost as a result of the abortion and the surgery. After a moment of thought, she indicated that she had also lost her old self-image. She felt she could never again be the naive idealist she had been to that point. She had done something she would previously have thought unimaginable, and if she could do this, she thought, anyone could do anything. This was a shattering experience for her. It changed not only how she viewed herself but also how she viewed everyone else. She described it as the loss of innocence or the end of childhood. She also said that this loss of her former self-image was unquestionably part of her sadness, though she had not been able to put it into words until that very moment. Then came the following interchange:

Pastor: As I listen to you talk, it becomes increasingly clear why you are feeling so sad. You have lost so much in the past weeks and months. You lost your innocence, something of your idealism, and your way of thinking about yourself and the world. You also lost important parts of your body, and this too is a most significant emotional loss. But on top of that, of course, you also lost the capacity to bear children, and this is an enormous loss for you. You are like someone who has just suffered the death of a very close loved one and then a few weeks later loses yet another loved one. Your grief is the compounded result of each of those losses. But it seems to me to be normal and even healthy. In fact, I'd be more concerned for you if you were not feeling sad. Your sadness will decrease with time, particularly as you continue to face the underlying feelings and deal with the losses. But right now the feelings are a realistic response to real losses.

Ellen: [Laughing.] I'm not sure if that makes me feel better or worse. But I guess it's good to hear that what I'm feeling is normal. I've been depressed, and then I've been getting down on myself for feeling that way. That has only made me feel worse.

Commentary: The pastor's intervention here was designed to help Ellen normalize her experience. Counselors need to be careful neither to normalize things that are abnormal nor to treat as abnormal things that are normal. But Ellen's grief appears to be a normal reaction to a substantial loss. It is also important to recognize that the grieving process for a loss such as the one Ellen is facing involves grieving over each of the separate components of that loss. Thus, the pastor attempted to identify the elements of Ellen's loss in order to help her deal with each separately.

Following this discussion, Ellen switched the topic to her husband, reporting that she had talked with him about marital counseling and that he had become furious with her for suggesting that they had problems. He told her that the problem was all hers and that she should see a psychiatrist if she wanted to talk more about it. Ellen had been somewhat prepared for this response but still found it devastating. She expressed her anger at him for his treatment of her and then found herself again caught in feelings of sadness about the prospects for the marriage. The pastor then asked her if she had ideas about how to handle this situation. She professed hopelessness and asked him what she should do. He declined to answer, asking her to brainstorm about her possibilities. While she seemed to have considerable trouble with this, she slowly began to identify things she could do that might help her husband become less defensive and that might help their communication. The pastor encouraged her to identify several specific goals from among them to work on before the next session and ended by setting the date for the final session (three weeks later). He also indicated that they would use the last session to review progress, briefly consider any remaining concerns (including her relationship with her father if she still wished to discuss this further), and together look ahead to the future.

Commentary: The pastor's intervention concerning the discussion of Ellen's marriage was a good way of dealing with this matter. As already identified, her marital problems went beyond the reasonable focus of the five sessions. However, it was appropriate, particularly as they prepared for the termination of counseling, to plan for things Ellen could do apart from the counseling sessions. The pastor discouraged dependence on him by refusing to tell her what she should do about her marriage and by encouraging her to set realistic goals and to try to implement them before the final session.

Fifth Session (Three Weeks Later)

Ellen began the final session by talking about some of the things she had tried to do to improve communication with her husband. These efforts had been moderately successful. She and her husband had had a reasonably good conversation about her feelings concerning the hysterectomy. While he had become upset at her suggestion that perhaps when the time was right they could consider adopting children, she did feel that he had some understanding of her feelings. However, nothing else seemed to have changed in the marriage.

The pastor then asked her if she had come with other matters she wanted to discuss or if she had reflected on their work together. She said she had thought about their four previous sessions and felt they had been enormously helpful. When asked if she could be more specific, she indicated that the most important thing the pastor had done for her was to accept her feelings and help her to do the same. She also said that her feelings had changed quite a bit since she had first consulted him. She continued to experience God's forgiveness and had never really doubted this in recent weeks. However, while her feelings of guilt and depression were better, she was still feeling quite a bit of anger, mostly at her husband. This led to the following:

Pastor: Well, tell me a bit about this anger. When do you feel it most?

Ellen: I guess I am angry most of the time. I feel it most when I'm with him. I just see how selfish he is. He is so like my father. I had never seen that as clearly as now. Neither of them can see past their own interests. Now I am beginning to understand how my mother must feel. I don't know how she has stayed with my father so long. I really feel sorry for her.

Pastor: I suspect you are right about there being some important similarities between your father and your husband. And because of that, it's certainly possible that some of your anger at your husband is a spillover of feelings that belong more appropriately to your father. I wonder if you have any sense of that being true.

Ellen: You may be right. I just know that the way he relates to me feels pretty familiar. I don't feel he sees me or even knows me in my own right. He sees me only as an extension of himself. And that is exactly the way I have always felt about my dad. When I first met Rick, he didn't seem at all like my dad, but now I see that the differences are relatively superficial. Basically, neither of them knows how to love anyone other than himself.

130

Pastor: That may be true. But I'm suggesting that you need to be careful to ensure that you are seeing your husband for who he is and not merely through your father-colored glasses. It seems to me that it must be awfully easy to fall into this trap, maybe impossible not to. But if you can be aware of this, it may help you encounter your husband for himself and not react to old conflicts with your father as you relate to your husband.

Commentary: Here the pastor was returning to the issue he had identified at the end of the second session, that is, the parallels in her relationships. His goal in these interventions was to help Ellen recognize the way in which her feelings in relation to her father might be contaminating her perception of and her relationship with her husband. If she became aware of this, she would be able to relate more realistically to her husband. The marital problem seemed to be the major outstanding problem, and the pastor was using this final session to help Ellen see some directions in which she could go after counseling.

The pastor then asked Ellen if she had other ideas about how she wanted to deal with her husband. She said she was convinced that they needed to see a marital counselor, but she had very little hope that her husband would ever agree to this. She went on to say that she had very little hope that he would change in any way. The pastor asked her to assume for a minute that her husband would not change and to consider how she would deal with this.

Ellen: Well, I guess I could just ignore him. If I keep trying to make the marriage better and he doesn't change, I'll just get more and more frustrated.

Pastor: That's possibly true, but I'm not sure that the only answers are to ignore him or to give up trying to improve the marriage. Another possibility is to limit what you expect from him. If you demand that he be a sensitive, emotionally supportive, and loving husband, you may be frustrated. But isn't it possible that you could have a good marriage without those things? It would definitely not be an ideal marriage, but couldn't it possibly be a workable one?

Ellen: But that isn't fair! I deserve better than that! I deserve real love. And I deserve a husband who is willing to communicate with me.

Pastor: You're right on both accounts. It isn't fair, and you do deserve better. But I asked how you would cope if things didn't change with your husband. I'm not saying that they won't. But I'm asking you to be realistic and to consider for the moment the possibility that he may not change in any significant way.

Ellen: I'm not sure that I could take that. Well, I guess I could, but I'm not sure that I want to. I think I could expect less of him, but I don't think that I'm ready to let him off that easy.

Pastor: But who are you really punishing by demanding that he be someone other than himself? Who is it hurting more, him or you?

Ellen: It's definitely hurting me more than him. So maybe you're right. Maybe I do need to change what I expect of him. I guess I should think about that some more.

Pastor: I think you should. If you could modify some of your expectations, I suspect you might feel less angry at him. At present, part of your anger is related to your demand that he be somebody he is not. You are asking him to change. He may not be able to make the changes you demand.

Ellen: I suspect that is true. That's one of the things that makes me feel most hopeless about the marriage.

Pastor: Apart from expecting less from him, I wonder what other ideas you have about how to relate to your husband. Could your faith provide any resources for coping with a less-than-satisfactory marriage?

Ellen: Well, my Christian beliefs tell me that I need to forgive him for the things he has done to me in the past. And I suspect I am going to have to continue to do that in the future. But I don't know that I can.

Pastor: I think you are right about both how hard that forgiveness is and yet how important it will be for both you and him. He may not even know what you need to forgive him for. You can't wait for him to come begging for forgiveness. But by God's help that is one very big thing that you can do. And maybe it will be easier for you now that you yourself have received God's forgiveness. Realizing we need God's forgiveness and then experiencing that forgiveness is often a great help in forgiving others. I suspect that you are well on your way toward being ready to forgive your husband for things he has done to you in the past, and I also think you are being realistic when you acknowledge that this won't be the last time you will need to do this.

At this point, the pastor also suggested that Ellen not give up on the idea of marital counseling nor to interpret his comments as suggesting that changes in her husband or their marriage were impossible. He also indicated that even if her husband would not go with her to see a marital counselor, she might want to consider going for herself. He offered once more to help her contact a marital counselor if this was what she desired.

Noting that they were approaching the end of the session, the pastor asked Ellen how she felt about the counseling relationship drawing to a close. She said she felt a little sad, as she had found the sessions to be very helpful. She said that today's session had been particularly helpful and that she wished she could talk further with him about these matters. He responded that it was necessary to end the counseling relationship as they had planned but that if, after a passage of time, she ever wished to return to see him again, she should certainly feel free to call and set up an appointment. He told her that he shared some of her sadness about discontinuing their meetings, as he had enjoyed their work together. He then asked if she would like him to offer a closing prayer of blessing, which she gratefully accepted.

Commentary: This final session illustrates the work of stage 3 of strategic pastoral counseling. Counseling ended at this point, even though Ellen expressed a desire to continue to meet and still faced some serious problems. But she had received significant help with the problems that had brought her to counseling, and she had received the distinctive help of pastoral counseling. If she chose to consult another counselor, she would do so with a foundation laid by this counseling experience.

No one case history can typify counseling of any sort. Ellen's experience was the experience of one particular parishioner with one particular pastor at one particular time. With some people, the tone of the sessions is much more emotional, with others more didactic and cognitive, and with still others more concrete and behavioral. And these emphases differ for different pastoral counselors as well as for the same pastoral counselor at different times.

What is typical of Ellen's case, however, is that a person struggling with life experiences consulted a pastor who functioned as a representative of Christ and who received her as such. What he gave her was his time, his attention, and his skill in therapeutic conversation. But more important, he brought her into contact with God and with the spiritual resources of the Christian life. This is the source of the dynamic power of strategic pastoral counseling. Its potency does not lie primarily in the technical interventions of the counselor but in the person of Christ and the healing, sustaining, and reconciling power of his Spirit.

6

Bill: A Single-Session Case Illustration

Pastors often think of counseling as an ongoing relationship, failing to realize that it can frequently be conducted within a single session. This is particularly true of strategic pastoral counseling, which, because of its focused nature, is extremely well suited to the needs of someone who wants a brief pastoral consultation rather than an ongoing counseling experience. This case illustration shows how a single session of counseling can cover the major tasks of the strategic pastoral counseling model and can bring a pastoral presence to someone seeking help.

Bill[1] was a forty-year-old married man and a long-standing member of the church. He and his wife were quite involved in the congregation, and their three children had grown up in it. Until recently, he had been the director of marketing for a Christian ministry involved in third world community development and disaster relief. Declining levels of financial

1. An abbreviated form of this case study was previously published by Benner and Harvey (1996).

135

support for the organization had recently led to the elimination of his position. Bill had received a six-month severance package and during those six months had been able to secure employment with an advertising firm doing similar work with considerably more compensation.

Bill had spoken briefly with the pastor on a couple of occasions about this transition. The present conversation began after church when the pastor asked him how his new job was going. This led to the following interaction:

Bill: The job is going pretty well, but I must admit I'm still having a hard time dealing with the way the last one ended.

Pastor: I'm sorry to hear that. In what way are you having a hard time?

Bill: I'm not sure now is the time to get into it. It's a bit hard to explain. Perhaps I should drop by your office some day and talk with you. Do you have any time this week? I don't think it would take long, but I'd love to get some of this off my chest.

Pastor: I'd be glad to get together. Why don't you let me give you a call tomorrow morning, and we will set a time to get together soon.

Commentary: If she were honest, the pastor would have to acknowledge that she had intended the question about work as more of a greeting than a serious inquiry. She was, therefore, somewhat surprised by Bill's response, but she recovered quickly and asked for more detail. This also did not produce the intended result, as Bill indicated that the time and setting were not right for an answer to her question. This made it clear that he was facing real struggles.

A few days later, Bill and the pastor met for their session.

Pastor: Good morning, Bill. I'm glad to see you.

Bill: Thanks. I'm really glad you asked me about my job. As I said, it's going well enough. It's actually pretty similar to what I was doing before. The only difference is that I'm not working for a Christian organization, and that is just fine with me right now. The problem isn't my new job. It's my feelings about the old one.

Pastor: Tell me a bit more about that.

Bill: Well, I'm still really upset about how they dumped me. In fact, in some ways I'm more upset now than I was six months ago when it happened. At the time, they told me that my termination had nothing to do with me. It was simply a matter of the reorganization making my department redundant. In fact, what they told me was that they would be using external ad agencies to do the work of our department and that this would be more cost effective for the organization. They may have done this for a while, but I just learned that they recently hired someone to do most of the things I was doing. I don't think this person is at the level I was at, but it still makes me upset to think that they fired me—telling me it had nothing to do with me but then turning around and hiring someone to do my job.

Pastor: That really is upsetting. It must make you feel betrayed. It can't help but look as if they were not being totally straight with you.

Bill: That's it exactly. And they are supposed to be Christians! That's the part that really gets me. That's the last time I will ever work for a Christian organization. I'll take my chances with the wolves any day. Save me from the sheep!

Pastor: It sounds as if a good part of your hurt is your disappointment with how they acted as Christians. You expected more from the organization because of that. You got bit by the sheep when all along you had been led to believe that the wolves did the biting.

Commentary: These first few minutes of the session allowed Bill and the pastor to get well into the tasks of the encounter stage of strategic pastoral counseling. Because of their prior relationship, joining was immediate. The pastor had done the necessary boundary setting during the phone conversation prior to the session. She had indicated that she had an hour to spend with him and that she looked forward to hearing more about his concerns and working with him to try to put them in perspective. Because these things had been taken care of, the pastor and parishioner were able to move rapidly into the exploration of the central concern.

Bill: That's what really hurts. They talk a good line, but what you see isn't what you get. They talk about building the organization on Christian values, but while I was there I saw so many people treated badly. I wasn't the first to be treated shamefully, and I probably won't be the last. If they simply wanted to replace me with someone less expensive, they should have told me that. But where is loyalty? I served them well for four years and did so while taking a big reduction in salary from what I could have been making. That was my commitment to them. Where was their commitment to me?

Pastor: Good question. But let's bring the focus back to you. Let's go back to why you took the position with the organization. I'm interested in hearing about the hopes you had about working in a Christian organization. I'm wondering if they are connected to your disappointment.

Commentary: This was a good intervention. It kept the focus on Bill, not on his former employer. It also introduced an important historical dimension to his problem and therefore related to the task of placing the present problems in a historical context. Finally, it introduced a line of discussion that would help the pastor better understand Bill's spiritual response to his dismissal and the bitterness he is experiencing.

In response to the pastor's question about why he had originally wanted to work for a Christian organization, Bill said that he wanted to serve God and make a difference in the world. He had previously held several jobs in secular adver-

138

tising firms and had been quite unhappy with his work. He had found himself troubled by the manipulative quality of the advertising industry and was about to leave the field and do something totally different when he was offered a position in this Christian organization. He said he was very excited about the opportunity to put his skills to use in a Christian setting. He was also interested in working with Christians because he thought he would be treated more fairly than people were treated in the places he had worked to that point.

Pastor: Were you treated unfairly in any of your previous positions?

Commentary: This was an excellent question. The pastor was trying to establish a background for Bill's present concerns. If Bill had a history of feeling unfairly treated by employers, there was a chance that he had contributed to this recent job failure.

Bill: Nothing as bad as in this last job. The company I was with the longest before this passed me over for a promotion that I really deserved and gave it to someone who was less qualified. I was disappointed at the time but eventually came to realize that you just can't count on fairness. I suppose that was a big part of why I wanted to work for a Christian organization. I was really hoping for something better than what I had experienced in other jobs.

Pastor: Does that feel like a part of a pattern in your life—feeling disappointed in others who aren't fair? Concluding that you just can't count on fairness sounds as if you had previous experience with this.

Bill: [After a long pause] I don't think I have ever thought of it as a pattern before, but it may just be. I certainly have had my share of experience with people who aren't fair, and I guess I do get disappointed in people quickly. I wish it wasn't true, but most people just don't seem to measure up to the standards they set for others, and I seem to see that sort of thing quickly and clearly. My wife has said that I have a nose for hypocrisy. It may be more of a curse than a blessing, but I think she is right.

Pastor: How have you reacted to this discovery that life isn't fair and that most people don't practice what they preach? Has it changed how you feel about the church or even God?

Commentary: This was another attempt to move toward the spiritual aspect of Bill's experience. The pastor wanted to do more than conduct a clinical interview. She wanted to identify the spiritual implications of his struggles and the spiritual resources that might be most helpful to him.

Bill: I'm afraid it has. I try not to generalize, but if I am honest, I have to admit that I do expect less from Christians. And although I don't think of myself as angry at God, I think I feel less close to him. I think the whole experience has made me pull into myself and away from people. Maybe I have also pulled back from God, although I haven't been aware of doing so. I guess I am just a bit self-preoccupied—at least that's what my wife tells me.

Pastor: And yet you reached out to me, telling me about your struggles and asking if we could talk. So you haven't totally given up on the church or other people.

Bill: That's true. I guess I answered your question as honestly as I did because I don't like what I see happening to me. I don't like the anger I feel at my former boss, I don't like the way it makes me bitter about Christian organizations, I don't like the way it makes me mistrustful of all Christians, and I don't like the way it makes me feel distant from God.

Pastor: Which of those would you like to focus on with me now?

Commentary: This was a good question. Without it, the pastor may have set the direction for the interview according to what she thought was most important. But Bill deserves to shape this conversation around what he thinks is most important. That is the essence of counseling and a major difference between counseling and most other forms of pastoral ministry.

Bill: Well, I suppose the right answer is my feelings about God, but actually I feel I need the most help with my feelings about my former boss. That's where I really feel stuck.

Pastor: Then that's absolutely where we should focus. Tell me what you mean when you say you feel stuck.

Bill replied by saying that he had tried to forgive his former boss but continued to feel angry. When asked what he had tried to forgive, he spoke in generalities. The pastor then suggested that he take a few moments and list the specific things that he felt he had lost as a result of the dismissal.[2] This turned out to be quite helpful. His list included the following:

- My sense of competence—this was my first real failure in life
- A number of friends—because I no longer see them at work, I have lost contact with them
- The feeling of making a difference in the world
- The ability to spend my day working on things that are important to my Christian commitment
- My hopefulness about the difference that being a Christian can make in a person
- My ability to trust people

2. This is a good example of the emotional work of the encounter stage. Anger that a person cannot release in forgiveness is often associated with unresolved grieving over things lost during a hurtful transaction. The pastor reveals a good understanding of this principle by her question at this point.

The pastor then asked him which of these felt like the most significant loss.

Bill: No question about that. It's my disappointment in the difference that being a Christian seems to make in life. It really saddens me to have to acknowledge this, but it seems that we have been deluded by our own rhetoric. Faith may make a difference in our relationship with God, but it really doesn't seem to make much of a difference with regard to who people are and how they relate to others. I wish it were otherwise, but I now have trouble believing that it does.

Pastor: Of all the things you feel you lost as a result of being fired, this feels like your greatest loss. Genuine spiritual change now seems like a naive hope. But if that is true, it must be really sad for you.

Bill: That's what really makes me feel most sad. I think I know that my feelings are not a good reflection of reality, but I have lost hope.

Pastor: What would restore that hope to you?

Bill: I guess I would need to see real changes in someone—and I mean *real* changes.

Pastor: What would real changes look like in you?

Commentary: This was a good question. It moved the discussion from useless abstractions (the kind of changes that in general would be convincing) to personal specifics (the kind of changes in himself that he most deeply longs for).

Bill: Wow. Is that a good question! [After a long pause] I guess I'd need to experience God's help in really forgiving my former boss. That's what I really want to do, but that's where I have felt so stuck.

Pastor: If you feel like that's something you really want, how would you feel about us taking a moment to pray to ask for the help you feel you need?

Bill: I'd like that.

The pastor then offered a brief prayer. She included a request that Bill be granted the gift of knowing what it is to be forgiven so that he would know what it is to forgive. They then began to talk again.

Bill: I found it interesting when you asked that I would know what it is to be forgiven. What I suddenly realized is that God must feel the same toward me as I do toward my former boss. I disappoint God and fail to meet his expectations of me even now as I'm having such a hard time forgiving someone else. But as soon as I see myself needing God's forgiveness, I know that I am forgiven. I really have no doubt about that. And because I am forgiven, I can offer the same forgiveness to someone else. That really makes all the difference in the world.

Pastor: I think it does. When I have trouble forgiving someone for something they have done to me, I find myself rushing back to God to receive his forgiveness of me. And then I remember what forgiveness is—passing on to others God's love, which he has already extended to me.

Bill: I'm ready to do that. In fact, I feel I already have.

Pastor: If so, are you willing to translate that into a prayer for this person? You don't even have to pray out loud, but you really can't hold on to your anger and at the same time pray for his blessing. Is that something you are ready to do?

Bill: Absolutely, and I'd like to pray that prayer out loud with you right now.

After doing so, the pastor asked Bill if he felt he had received the help he was hoping for when he asked to speak to her or if there was some other way in which she could be of help. He said that he felt the session had been extremely helpful and that there really wasn't anything more he wanted. He offered to let the pastor know how things were going but said he already felt a shift in his relationship with God and the church that told him his forgiveness had been genuine. The pastor responded by saying that even though it was undoubtedly genuine, it may not be final. She encouraged him to be prepared to face further feelings of resentment with the same act of release and prayer for the blessing of his former boss. They then ended the session.

When Bill next spoke to the pastor several weeks later, he told her that the session had been the breakthrough he had needed. He said he still occasionally felt sorry for himself and once or twice had felt anger when he thought about the situation or his former boss. However, those feelings were not as strong as they had been, and he had been able to release each new wave of disappointment or anger as it had washed over him. He also said he continued to feel closer to God and was particularly savoring the awareness of what it means to be forgiven by God.

Much of the counseling pastors do does not fit within the structure of the counseling relationship described by mental-health counselors. Meetings are often not by scheduled appointment. They are frequently more informal and do not always take place in an office. Parishioners may even end the interaction without being aware that they were "in counseling." And very often the encounter is less than forty minutes in length.

Strategic pastoral counseling fits well with these shorter, less formal counseling encounters. Once a pastor has internalized the basic structure of the model, he or she can implement it in a variety of ways.

Pastors need to learn to use the brief "counseling" conversations they already regularly have rather than seek to move people into a more formal counseling relationship. Strategic pastoral counseling allows pastors to do just that. At the same time, it also provides a useful framework for pastors who conduct counseling within a more traditional structure involving multiple scheduled appointments. The point is that counseling cannot be limited to either of these formats. Strategic pastoral counseling fits both equally well.

Ethical Considerations in Pastoral Counseling

Pastoral counselors, no less than any other counselors, must be attentive to the ethical concerns associated with counseling. Those who are members of a professional counseling organization (i.e., the American Association of Pastoral Counselors, the American Association of Marriage and Family Therapists, the American Psychological Association, or the Christian Association of Psychological Studies) are already accountable to the ethical code of that organization. However, all pastors who counsel—whether they have such memberships or not—need to be familiar with the ethical framework of counseling.

Codes of ethical conduct developed by major counseling organizations have a good deal in common. However, codes of ethical conduct developed by pastoral counselors are especially helpful for pastors. I personally recommend the code of ethics of the American Association of Pastoral Counselors and encourage all pastoral counselors to be familiar with it. It can be found on the internet at www.aapc.org/ethics.htm.

The following five guidelines, while not comprehensive, serve as a framework for the ethical practice of pastoral counseling:

1. *Protect the rights of those you counsel.* This includes but is not limited to the right to informed consent to all aspects of the work undertaken together, the right to self-determination and freedom from any form of manipulation or coercion, the right to freedom from harassment or discrimination, the right to freedom from unnecessary or prurient invasion of privacy, and the right to protection of confidentiality.

2. *Avoid dual role relationships.* One of the ways in which counselors can protect the rights of those they counsel is to avoid counseling someone with whom they have a close friendship, business or work relationship, or any other type of ongoing interaction. Such people should be referred to someone else, despite any protest they may have.

3. *Avoid romantic or sexual intimacies in counseling.* This guideline may seem obvious, but violation of this basic ethical boundary remains alarmingly common. There is absolutely no excuse for this form of exploitation, and any movement toward the boundary demands an immediate end to the counseling relationship.

4. *Be aware of your limitations.* All counselors have limitations. Ethical counselors are alert to them and take care not to operate outside their sphere of competence. A pastor can stay within this sphere of competence through consultation, supervision, and making appropriate referrals.

5. *Remain in relationships of personal accountability.* The ethical practice of counseling is best achieved and maintained within a context of close accountability, not merely familiarity with standards and guidelines. Such relationships should begin within the church and faith

community but should also extend to membership in professional counseling organizations such as the American Association of Pastoral Counselors. Accountability can also be achieved through ongoing consultation and supervision with other experienced counselors. Ideally, such relationships involve other pastoral counselors, but potential relationships with other experienced counselors and psychotherapists should not be overlooked.

References

Adams, J. 1970. *Competent to counsel.* Grand Rapids: Baker.

Aden, L. 1988. Pastoral care and the gospel. In *The church and pastoral care,* edited by L. Aden and J. Harold Ellens. Grand Rapids: Baker.

Aden, L., and J. H. Ellens, eds. 1988. *The church and pastoral care.* Grand Rapids: Baker.

Allen, D. 1981. *The traces of God in a frequently hostile world.* Cambridge, Mass.: Cowley Publications.

Benner, D. 1983. The incarnation as a metaphor for psychotherapy. *Journal of Psychology and Theology* 11:287–94.

———. 1988. *Psychotherapy and the spiritual quest.* Grand Rapids: Baker.

———. 1998. *Care of souls: Revisioning Christian nurture and counsel.* Grand Rapids: Baker.

———. 1999. Fees for psychotherapy. In *Baker encyclopedia of psychology and counseling,* edited by D. Benner and P. Hill. 2d ed. Grand Rapids: Baker.

———. 2002. *Sacred companions: The gift of spiritual friendship and direction.* Downers Grove, Ill.: InterVarsity.

Benner, D., and R. Harvey. 1996. *Understanding and facilitating forgiveness.* Grand Rapids: Baker.

Buber, M. 1965. *The knowledge of man.* London: George Allen & Unwin.

Campbell, A. 1985. *Paid to care: The limits of professionalism in pastoral care.* London: SPCK.

Childs, B. 1990. *Short-term pastoral counseling.* Nashville: Abingdon.

151

References

Clebsch, W., and C. Jaekle. 1964. *Pastoral care in historical perspective*. Englewood Cliffs, N.J.: Prentice-Hall.

Clinebell, H. 1984. *Basic types of pastoral care and counseling*. Nashville: Abingdon.

Close, H. 1998. Pastoral care for an unconscious person. *Journal of Pastoral Care* 52, no. 2:175–81.

Crabb, L. 1977. *Effective biblical counseling*. Grand Rapids: Zondervan.

———. 1997. *Connecting: Healing for ourselves and our relationships*. Nashville: Word.

———. 2002. *The pressure's off*. Colorado Springs: WaterBrook Press.

Danco, J. 1982. The ethics of fee practices: An analysis of presuppositions and accountability. *Journal of Psychology and Theology* 10:13–21.

Eschmann, H. 2000. Toward a pastoral care in a trinitarian perspective. *Journal of Pastoral Care* 54, no. 4:419–27.

Fénelon, F. 1980. *Spiritual letters to women*. New Canaan, Conn.: Keats.

Galindo, I. 1997. Spiritual direction and pastoral counseling: Addressing the needs of the spirit. *Journal of Pastoral Care* 51, no. 4:395–402.

Gurin, G., J. Verhoff, and S. Feld. 1960. *Americans view their mental health*. New York: Basic Books.

Hill, P. 1999. Religious health and pathology. In *Baker encyclopedia of psychology and counseling*, edited by D. Benner and P. Hill. 2d ed. Grand Rapids: Baker.

Hiltner, S., and L. Colston. 1961. *The context of pastoral counseling*. New York: Abingdon.

Holifield, E. B. 1983. *A history of pastoral care in America*. Nashville: Abingdon.

Hulme, W. 1981. *Pastoral care and counseling*. Minneapolis: Augsburg.

James, W. 1902. *The varieties of religious experience*. New York: Longman, Green.

Kollar, C. 1997. *Solution-focused pastoral counseling*. Grand Rapids: Zondervan.

Lambert, M. J., and A. E. Bergin. 1994. The effectiveness of psychotherapy. In *Handbook of psychotherapy and behavior change*, edited by S. Garfield and A. Bergin. New York: Wiley.

Lewis, C. S. 1940. *The problem of pain*. London: Collins.

———. 1961. *A grief observed*. New York: Bantam Books.

Malony, H. N. 1985. Assessing religious maturity. In *Psychotherapy and the religiously committed patient*, edited by E. M. Stern. New York: Hayworth.

———. 1988. The clinical assessment of optimal religious functioning. *Review of Religious Research* 30, no. 1:2–17.

Manning, B. 1990. *The ragamuffin gospel*. Sisters, Ore.: Multnomah.

May, G. 1982. *Will and spirit*. San Francisco: Harper & Row.

McNeil, J. 1951. *A history of the cure of souls*. New York: Harper & Row.

Nessan, C. 1998. Confidentiality: Sacred trust and ethical quagmire. *Journal of Pastoral Care* 52, no. 4:349–57.

Nouwen, H. 1994. *Return of the prodigal son*. New York: Doubleday.

Oates, W. 1962. *Protestant pastoral counseling*. Philadelphia: Westminster.

———. 1970. *When religion gets sick*. Philadelphia: Westminster.

References

Oden, T. 1966. *Kerygma and counseling.* Philadelphia: Westminster.
————. 1984. *Care of souls in the classic tradition.* Philadelphia: Fortress.
Olthius, J. 1989. The covenanting metaphor of the Christian faith and the self psychology of Heinz Kohut. *Studies in Religion/Sciences Religieuses* 18, no. 3:313–24.
Peterson, E. 2002. *A long obedience in the same direction.* Downers Grove, Ill.: InterVarsity.
Propst, L. R. 1988. *Psychotherapy in a religious framework: Spirituality in the emotional healing process.* New York: Human Sciences.
Pruyser, P. 1976. *The minister as diagnostician.* Philadelphia: Westminster.
Rieff, P. 1966. *The triumph of the therapeutic.* New York: Harper & Row.
Rogers, C. 1961. *On becoming a person.* Boston: Houghton Mifflin.
Rohr, R. 1999. *Everything belongs: The gift of contemplative prayer.* New York: Crossroad.
Sharp, J. 1999. Solution-focused counseling: A model for parish ministry. *Journal of Pastoral Care* 53, no. 1:71–79.
Shea, J. J. 1997. Adult faith, pastoral counseling, and spiritual direction. *Journal of Pastoral Care* 51, no. 3:259–70.
Smedes, L. 1984. *Forgive and forget: Healing the hurts we don't deserve.* New York: Pocket Books.
Stone, H. 1994. *Brief pastoral counseling: Short-term approaches and strategies.* Minneapolis: Fortress.
————. 1999. Pastoral counseling and the changing times. *Journal of Pastoral Care* 53, no. 1:31–45.
————, ed. 2001. *Strategies for brief pastoral counseling.* Minneapolis: Fortress.
Tan, S. Y. 1999. Cognitive-behavior therapy. In *Baker encyclopedia of psychology and counseling,* edited by D. Benner and P. Hill. 2d ed. Grand Rapids: Baker.
Tan, S. Y., and J. Ortberg. 1995. *Understanding depression.* Grand Rapids: Baker.
Thomas, F. 1999. Competency-based relationship counseling: The necessity of goal setting and counselor flexibility in efficient and effective couple counseling. *Journal of Pastoral Care* 53, no. 1:87–99.
Tozer, A. W. 1993. *The pursuit of God.* Camp Hill, Pa.: Christian Publications.
Verhoff, J., R. Kukla, and E. Dorran. 1981. *Mental health in America.* New York: Basic Books.
Wicks, R., R. Parsons, and D. Capps, eds. 1985. *Clinical handbook of pastoral counseling.* New York: Paulist Press.
Westberg, G. 1979. *Theological roots of wholistic health care.* Hinsdale, Ill.: Wholistic Health Centers.
Yancey, P. 1988. *Disappointment with God.* Grand Rapids: Zondervan.

Dr. David G. Benner is an internationally known author, lecturer, and retreat director. For the past thirty years, his work has focused on the development and practice of a spiritually sensitive depth psychology and the nurture of a psychologically grounded Christian spirituality. His educational background includes an Honors B.A. in psychology (McMaster University), an M.A. and a Ph.D. in clinical psychology (York University), and postdoctoral studies at the Chicago Institute of Psychoanalysis. He has authored or edited twenty books, including *Surrender to Love, Sacred Companions, Baker Encyclopedia of Psychology and Counseling, Care of Souls, Free at Last, Understanding and Facilitating Forgiveness, Choosing the Gift of Forgiveness, Christian Perspectives on Human Development, Psychotherapy and the Spiritual Quest, Psychology and Religion,* and *Christian Counseling and Psychotherapy.*

Dr. Benner has held numerous clinical and academic appointments in Canada, the United States, and abroad. North American faculty appointments have included York University, University of Toronto, Tyndale College and Seminary, McMaster University Divinity College, Redeemer University College, and Wheaton College. He has also served as visiting lecturer at Charles University (Prague), the University of Cape Town (South Africa), and Rhodes University (South Africa). Clinical appointments have included serving as senior psychologist at Queen Street Mental Health Centre (Toronto), clinical director for the Institute for Eating Disorders (Carol Stream, Illinois), and consulting psychologist to the Children in War Zones Program of the Centre for International Health (McMaster University).

He currently serves as Distinguished Professor of Psychology and Spirituality at the Psychological Studies Institute (Atlanta), chief psychologist at Child and Adolescent Services (Hamilton, Ontario), and retreat leader and lecturer at the Tao Fong Shan Christian Centre (Hong Kong). He is also the founding director of the Institute for Psychospiritual Health. Dr. Benner and his wife reside in Hamilton, Ontario, dividing their time between there, Atlanta, and Asia.